HOPE UNDER CONSTRUCTION

INSIGHTS INTO THE LIFE OF NEHEMIAH

GENE GETZ

MEN of PURPOSE

BY SERENDIPITY HOUSE

LifeWay | Small Groups

Published by Serendipity House Publishers
Nashville, Tennessee

ISBN: 1-5749-4172-0
Item 001272940

Dewey Decimal Classification: 248.842
Subject Headings:
NEHEMIAH \ MEN \ CHRISTIAN LIFE

To purchase additional copies of this resource or other studies:
ORDER ONLINE at www.SerendipityHouse.com;
WRITE Serendipity House, One LifeWay Plaza, Nashville, TN 37234-0175
FAX (615) 251-5933

1-800-458-2772
www.SerendipityHouse.com

CONTENTS

HOPE UNDER CONSTRUCTION

HOPE UNDER CONSTRUCTION

A STUDY OF THE LIFE OF NEHEMIAH

Meet one of the greatest leaders of all time—Nehemiah. Although he had *every reason on earth* to lose hope and give up, Nehemiah knew he had access to *every resource in heaven* to bring to bear on his earthly crises. Whether you want to be a stronger and more effective leader in your home, business, church, or community, Nehemiah can teach you the leadership principles that will work in every situation. Nehemiah faced an impossible task on an impossible deadline ... opposition, false accusations and ridicule from his enemies ... betrayal ... personal and team discouragement ... and even conflict and sinful rebellion among his own people. Nehemiah's balance between wholeheartedly trusting God and fiercely exerting his own initiative provides us all with a model of how to demolish discouragement and emerge victorious no matter what we're facing!

The Men of Purpose series focuses on the lives of men in the Bible who provide poignant examples of godly masculinity. Each of these leaders faced trials, frustration, and failure, yet was inspired by God to achieve great goals. In a world where Christian male role models seem increasingly rare, this series reminds us that some of the most worthy examples of godly character can be found in the biblical figures who brought power, wisdom, and inspiration to God's people throughout the ages.

As you and your group approach each study, do so with the same spiritual passion and personal integrity that have characterized Dr. Getz throughout his lifetime. Let the goals of every group meeting be to understand biblical truths, to grapple with Dr. Getz' principles to live by, and to commit to helping each other apply what you learn in your daily lives. This is the supreme act of a disciple—being doers of God's Word (James 1:22-25).

HOW TO USE THIS BOOK

While this Bible study may be used individually, it is designed to be used within the context of small groups. Each group meeting should include all elements of the following "three-part agenda."

Icebreaker: Fun, history-giving questions are designed to warm up the group and build understanding between group members. You may choose

4

to use all of the Icebreaker questions, especially if there is a new group member that will need help in feeling comfortable with the group.

One of the purposes of this book is to begin and to then solidify a group. Therefore, getting to know one another and bonding together are essential to the success of this effort. The Icebreaker segment in each group session is designed to help you become better acquainted, greatly enhancing your group experience.

Bible Study: The heart of each meeting is your examination together of the Bible and the key "Principles to Live By" that are drawn from the Bible. This section emphasizes understanding what the Bible says and applying its truth to real life. The questions are open discovery questions that lead to further inquiry. Reference notes are provided to give everyone a "level playing field" and provide deeper insights into the biblical story. The questions for each session build on one another. There are always "going deeper" questions provided. You should always leave time for the last of the "questions for interaction." You may elect to use the optional "going deeper" questions to lead you in applying what the group has learned. This segment also satisfies the desire for more challenging questions in groups that have been together for a while.

To help your men connect as a group, it is important for everyone to participate in the Bible study. There are no right or wrong answers to the questions. Participants should strive to make all of the other group members feel comfortable during the Bible study time. Because we all have differing levels of biblical knowledge, it is essential that we understand and appreciate the personal context from which each one of us responds. We don't have to know much about theology and history to bring our own perspectives to bear on the truths contained in the Scriptures. It is vital that you keep encouraging all group members to share what they are observing as you work through these important Bible passages.

Caring Time: All study should lead us to action. Each session ends with prayer and direction in caring for the needs of individual group members. You can choose between the various questions provided, or use them all.

Small groups help the larger body of Christ in many ways: caring for individuals, holding one another up in prayer, providing emotional support, and bringing new men into the church family. Each week it is important to remember to pray for those whom God would bring to your group.

How to get the most out of this book ————————

Begin by reviewing the following ground rules and talk about the importance of "sharing your story" (see below).

Ground Rules

- **Priority**: While you are in the group, give the group meeting priority.

- **Participation**: Everyone participates and no one dominates.

- **Respect**: Everyone is given the right to his own opinion and all questions are encouraged ... and respected.

- **Confidentiality**: Anything that is said in the meeting is never repeated outside the meeting.

- **Empty Chair**: The group stays open to inviting new men to every meeting. Keeping an empty chair in your circle symbolizes those men you need to invite.

- **Support**: Permission is given to call upon each other in time of need— even in the middle of the night.

- **Advice Giving**: Unsolicited advice is not allowed.

- **Mission**: We agree to do everything in our power to work toward starting a new group—a vital part of our mission.

Sharing Your Story ————————

These sessions are designed to assist group members to share a little of their personal lives each time the group meets. Through a number of special techniques, each member is encouraged to move from low risk, less personal sharing to higher risk responses. This helps develop authentic community and facilitates care-giving within your group.

It is only when group members begin to share their own stories that the group bonds at levels deep enough for life-change to take place.

Personal Notes

LAYING THE FOUNDATION ... PRAYER

WELCOME

Though Nehemiah's life story does not occupy the same amount of space as some of the other Old Testament leaders God chose to influence Israel, Nehemiah certainly stands tall on the pages of Scripture. In fact, we can learn more about this man's specific leadership qualities and skills than we can about most of the better-known Bible characters. There are some individuals who have a special place in God's scheme of things—people God chooses to use in unique ways to achieve His purposes. Nehemiah is one of those special people.

One of the leadership skills that we will see in Nehemiah is his approach to prayer when faced with what appeared to be an impossible task. We will consider how to use his "prayer process" as a model when difficult challenges confront us in our own lives and ministries.

ICEBREAKER

Probably everyone in this group has known and admired a remarkable person who faced challenges with unusual courage and faith—someone who showed great leadership ability and helped those around him or her to see possibilities they could never have seen by themselves. Perhaps the person who comes to your mind was also a person who knew how to pray effectively. If so, you are thinking of someone like Nehemiah.

1. Who has been the most inspirational leader you've ever known? What impressed you most about that person?

2. What did your inspirational leader help people to do? What was unusual about that?

3. If your inspirational leader was a spiritual person, what role did spirituality play in his or her greatness?

Sometime after the Jews began to return from Babylon to the land of Israel, a man named Nehemiah caught the eye of King Artaxerxes, the emperor of Persia. He became the mighty monarch's personal cupbearer—the man who tasted the emperor's wine and guarded his sleeping quarters. Artaxerxes no doubt also consulted him for advice and wisdom.

The very fact that Nehemiah occupied this role in the king's court demonstrates his sterling character. This pagan king would never trust a man who did not exemplify total honesty, trustworthiness, and outstanding wisdom. Nehemiah was this kind of man because he never abandoned the God of Abraham, Isaac, and Jacob. He had a great love for the Lord and committed himself to keeping the laws of God in spite of his pagan environment.

The Prayer That Started It All

[1] The words of Nehemiah son of Hacaliah: During the month of Chislev in the twentieth year, when I was in the fortress city of Susa, [2] Hanani, one of my brothers, arrived with men from Judah, and I questioned them about Jerusalem and the Jewish remnant that had returned from exile. [3] They said to me, "The survivors in the province, who returned from the exile, are in great trouble and disgrace. Jerusalem's wall has been broken down, and its gates have been burned down."

[4] When I heard these words, I sat down and wept. I mourned for a number of days, fasting and praying before the God of heaven. [5] I said, LORD God of heaven, the great and awe-inspiring God who keeps His gracious covenant with those who love Him and keep His commands, [6] let Your eyes be open and Your ears be attentive to hear Your servant's prayer that I now pray to You day and night for Your servants, the Israelites. I confess the sins we have committed against You. Both I and my father's house have sinned. [7] We have acted corruptly toward You and have not kept the commands, statutes, and ordinances You gave Your servant Moses. [8] Please remember what You commanded Your servant Moses: "[If] you are unfaithful, I will scatter you among the peoples. [9] But if you return to Me and carefully observe My commands, even though your exiles were banished to the ends of the earth, I will gather them from there and bring them to the place where I chose to have My name dwell." [10] They are Your servants and Your people. You redeemed [them] by Your great power and strong hand. [11] Please, Lord, let Your ear be attentive to the prayer of Your servant and to that of Your servants who delight to revere Your name. Give Your servant success today, and have compassion on him in the presence of this man. [At the time,] I was the king's cupbearer.

Nehemiah 1:1-11

LESSON 1

PRINCIPLES TO LIVE BY

Nehemiah reminds us that in our moments of pain and helplessness we have access to God, the One who can help us make our way through life's darkest moments. Nehemiah fleshes out the words of David who wrote, "Even when I go through the darkest valley, I fear no danger, for You are with me" (Ps. 23:4).

What makes Nehemiah's prayer so unique is that he outlines a process we can apply to our own lives during periods of crisis. Before we look at the specific steps in this process, we need to look at Nehemiah's attitudes and actions prior to the prayer itself. This is as important as the very words that flowed from his lips.

PRINCIPLE 1

LIKE NEHEMIAH, WE MUST PRAY OUT OF A HEART OF DEEP CONCERN.

Nehemiah was so distressed and emotionally distraught over the bad news about Jerusalem that he writes, "I sat down and wept. I mourned for a number of days" (Neh. 1:4). He doesn't say exactly how long this grieving went on, but it was four months before he acted on the news he received (2:1). He focused so much on the plight of his fellow Jews that he refused to eat, at least on a regular basis, and devoted hours and days to prayer. If we want to see results from our prayers, we need to consider whether we are willing to open our hearts to feel the kind of distress and compassion that motivated Nehemiah's prayers.

PRINCIPLE 2

LIKE NEHEMIAH, WE MUST MAKE PRAYER A PRIORITY OVER OTHER NEEDS.

The Bible often associates fasting with prayer. The purpose of fasting is not abstinence from food as a means of manipulating God. Rather, fasting demonstrates to God that we are willing to spend time talking to Him in place of meeting our ordinary physical needs. Though Nehemiah had access to the best food in the Persian Empire, he refrained from eating so he could devote his time to prayer. Day after day and week after week he poured out his soul before the Lord for his brothers and sisters in Jerusalem. Consequently, God's heart was deeply moved.

LIKE NEHEMIAH, WE MUST PRAY PERSISTENTLY.

Nehemiah's heart was so deeply moved with compassion for the suffering Jews in Jerusalem that he persisted in prayer day after day. Consequently God's own heart was touched. Jesus told a parable in which an unrighteous judge reluctantly responded to a poor widow's plea for justice because she hounded him to death (Luke 18:1-5). He reasoned that if a crooked magistrate would give in before persistence, how much more would God, the righteous judge, "grant justice to His elect who cry out to Him day and night" (v. 7). Nehemiah serves as an Old Testament illustration of the truth Jesus taught that day.

PRINCIPLE 4

LIKE NEHEMIAH, WE MUST RECOGNIZE THAT ALTHOUGH GOD IS OUR FRIEND, HE IS UNIMAGINABLY GREAT AND AWESOME.

In the midst of his own despair, Nehemiah lifted his heart upward and acknowledged God's unfathomable greatness, His incomparable power, His omniscience, His omnipresence, and His majesty. Only God could deal effectively with the troubles the residents of Jerusalem faced. We too should approach the holy, sovereign Lord of the universe with awe and reverence. God is our friend, but we should never take Him for granted. We can approach His awesome throne of grace because of the sacrifice of our Savior Jesus Christ.

PRINCIPLE 5

LIKE NEHEMIAH, WE SHOULD ALSO REFLECT ON AND REMIND GOD OF HIS PROMISES TO US.

Nehemiah prayed to the "LORD God of heaven . . . who keeps His gracious covenant with those who love Him and keep His commands" (Neh. 1:5). By using the divine name Yahweh (LORD), Nehemiah acknowledged that God never reneges on His promises. It pleases the Lord to hear His children reiterate His promises when they're talking with Him. He responds positively when we repeat in our prayers the things He has taught us and promised us. God enjoys and appreciates being heard.

LESSON 1

PRINCIPLE 6

LIKE NEHEMIAH, WE MUST ACKNOWLEDGE OUR UNWORTHINESS AND SINFULNESS, OUR HUMAN WEAKNESSES AND FAILINGS.

Nehemiah associated himself with Israel's sins. He didn't rationalize away his corporate connection to God's people who had failed Him as a nation. Nehemiah also used that corporate connection to remind God that he wasn't the only one confessing and desiring national renewal. Our salvation is secure in Christ because of the continual cleansing from sin His blood affords. However, if God is going to respond to our prayers, we must walk in fellowship with the Lord, free from deliberate sins. When we knowingly sin against God, we should ask for forgiveness, confident He has already granted it.

PRINCIPLE 7

LIKE NEHEMIAH, WE MUST BE SPECIFIC IN OUR PRAYERS IF WE WANT TO GET SPECIFIC ANSWERS.

During the prolonged period when Nehemiah prayed and fasted, God apparently made it clear to him that there was only one individual on earth who could encourage Nehemiah's fellow Jews in Jerusalem. That individual was King Artaxerxes, whom Nehemiah served. That's why Nehemiah prayed so specifically, "Give Your servant success today, and have compassion on him in the presence of this man" (Neh. 1:11b). Paul advised the Philippians, "Don't worry about anything, but in everything, through prayer and petition with thanksgiving, let your requests be made known to God" (Phil. 4:6). Everything that touches our lives is important to God. Nothing is too small; nothing is too big. Pray specifically.

Questions for Interaction

1. What life situations that we face can feel as though our "walls" are broken down and our "gates" are burned with fire?

2. When things are crumbling around them, what kinds of things do men tend to do instead of praying?

3. Nehemiah asked his brother from Jerusalem about the people and the place (Neh. 1:2). What did he learn about each (v. 3)?

4. Describe Nehemiah's response to the news about Jerusalem using only the information in verse 4.

5. What does Nehemiah's prayer say about God (vv. 5-11)?

6. What do you learn from Nehemiah's prayer about God's promises (vv. 8-10)?

7. Why did Nehemiah spend so much time on praise (v. 5-6a), confession (vv. 6b-7), and the promises of God (vv. 8-11a) and so little time on asking for what he wanted (v. 11b)?

8. If you wanted to pray more like Nehemiah, what would you have to give more time to? What would you need to give less time to?

Going Deeper

9. What are some life issues that move your heart to feel compassion like Nehemiah felt for Jerusalem?

10. What are some things you could do to focus your mind and your heart on a special prayer need over an extended period of time?

11. Why do you think God wants us to persist in prayer? Why doesn't He just answer immediately if it's in His will?

Caring Time

This Nehemiah study will give us unusual opportunities to draw close to one another in mutual care and support. Week after week we will observe Nehemiah in stressful leadership situations with which we'll all identify. It's appropriate that we meet this "man's man" on his knees. He can help us all wrestle with the big and small crises of our lives in ways that honor and please our heavenly Father.

1. Go around the group sharing the biggest problem looming out there that each guy would like to have some success in handling through this time of studying Nehemiah.

2. Focus on each man in turn and identify qualities or characteristics of God that can help him face his problem.

3. Close in a prayer time during which each man prays for a specific step of success for the guy to his right as he wrestles with his problem.

Next Week

Next week we will look behind the scenes to discover why Nehemiah was so concerned about how his boss, King Artaxerxes, would respond to his interest in the welfare of Jerusalem. Nehemiah knew he needed to do more than pray about the condition of his homeland. He had homework to do alongside his intense, persistent praying. Nehemiah can teach us several things about effective preparation for those big moments upon which success so often hinges.

LESSON 1

Scripture Notes

Nehemiah 1:1-11

1:1 Nehemiah. Probably born in Persia, he served as King Artaxerxes' personal cupbearer. He was also an important statesman who helped Ezra reestablish the Jews in Jerusalem. His name means "the Lord comforts." His great-grandparents may have been taken into captivity when the Babylonians captured Jerusalem.

the month of Chislev. The Jewish month Chislev corresponds roughly with December. Artaxerxes' twentieth year was 446 B.C. (perhaps 445 B.C.).

the fortress city of Susa. The capital of Persia, located nearly 300 miles east of Babylon and 150 miles north of the Persian Gulf in modern Iran.

1:2 Hanani, one of my brothers. Nehemiah's brother who brought him a message at the Persian palace. The troubling report said Jerusalem's wall was broken down and its gates were burned, making it vulnerable to attack. Nehemiah later appointed Hanani to an important position in Jerusalem (7:2).

1:4 fasting and praying. Going without food often indicated grief or an especially fervent prayer request (Ps. 35:13; 109:24).

1:6 servant's prayer that I now pray to You day and night. Nehemiah wept, fasted, and prayed continuously for several days over the condition of Jerusalem. He knew he could not solve the problem without God's help.

Both I and my father's house have sinned. He included himself and his family when he confessed the sins of the Israelites. He shared the responsibility for Israel's disobedience.

1:8 [If] you are unfaithful, I will scatter you. He reminded God of His covenant in Leviticus 26:27-45. If the Israelites were unfaithful, God would send them from their homeland to various places; but if they obeyed, He would regather them to Jerusalem (Deut. 30:1-5). Nehemiah recalled God's own words in his plea for help.

1:10 by Your great power and strong hand. Recalling God's work in the past (Ex. 32:11), Nehemiah asked Him to once again help the people. They belonged to God, and God would hear their prayers and help them. They needed God's power in their lives (Deut. 9:29).

CREATING WINDOWS FOR OPPORTUNITY

LAST WEEK

In the first lesson of this study, we saw Nehemiah devastated by some extremely bad news. His brother informed him that Jerusalem, the city of his ancestors, lay defenseless before its enemies. All the residents of the city were "in great trouble and disgrace" (Neh. 1:3). We saw this Jewish official in the court of the Persian Empire drop to his knees in prayer and start bombarding the throne of God during a four-month siege. We looked at the heart attitudes of Nehemiah that made his praying effective. He was a man of deep compassion who prioritized prayer over feeding his face. He persisted in praising God, confessing sin, claiming God's promises, and petitioning God for a specific answer. From the opening lines of the book bearing his name, Nehemiah challenges us to walk in his spiritual footsteps and look to God for the strength to carry out His will effectively.

ICEBREAKER

During a suspenseful story, we do not know what is going to happen. Tension builds in the plot as a crucial moment nears. We know that what the hero does at this moment determines whether he solves the mystery, cracks the spy ring, finds the buried treasure, or saves the heroine's life. In stories, we expect the hero to do just the right thing in the absolute nick of time. In real life, it is a lot harder to do the right thing at the right time.

1. What is your favorite in-the-nick-of-time heroic action in a movie or story? Why is it your favorite?

2. When you look back over your life, what incident stands out as an example of perfect timing—the right thing at the right time?

3. When you look back over your life, what incident stands out as an example of horrible timing—the wrong thing at the wrong time?

Nehemiah probably knew that the situation in Jerusalem was bad. He just didn't know how bad it had become. A few years earlier, a Syrian official named Rehum had convinced Artaxerxes to prohibit the Jews from rebuilding Jerusalem. His selling point had been that Jerusalem had a long history of rebelling against various emperors (Ezra 4:12-22). Rehum then used force to stop the reconstruction of Jerusalem (Ezra 4:23). When Hanani showed up in Susa (Neh. 1:1), Nehemiah found out just how much force Rehum had applied.

Rehum not only demoralized the Jews in Jerusalem at the time he destroyed the walls and burned the gates. This also demoralized Nehemiah when he heard about it years later and hundreds of miles away. However, Nehemiah did not wallow in his despair. He turned it over to God and, while he prayed, a plan started percolating through his mind and heart.

The Moment of Truth

[1] During the month of Nisan in the twentieth year of King Artaxerxes, when wine was set before him, I took the wine and gave it to the king. I had never been sad in his presence, [2] so the king said to me, "Why are you sad, when you aren't sick? This is nothing but sadness of heart."

I was overwhelmed with fear [3] and replied to the king, "May the king live forever! Why should I not be sad when the city where my ancestors are buried lies in ruins and its gates have been destroyed by fire?"

[4] Then the king asked me, "What is your request?"

So I prayed to the God of heaven [5] and answered the king, "If it pleases the king, and if your servant has found favor with you, send me to Judah and to the city where my ancestors are buried, so that I may rebuild it."

[6] The king, with the queen seated beside him, asked me, "How long will your journey take, and when will you return?" So I gave him a definite time, and it pleased the king to send me.

[7] I also said to the king: "If it pleases the king, let me have letters [written] to the governors of the region west of the Euphrates River, so that they will grant me [safe] passage until I reach Judah. [8] And [let me have] a letter [written] to Asaph, keeper of the king's forest, so that he will give me timber to rebuild the gates of the temple's fortress, the city wall, and the home where I will live." The king granted my [requests], for I was graciously strengthened by my God.

Nehemiah 2:1-8

LESSON 2

17

Principles to Live By

One of the greatest lessons we can learn from Nehemiah's approach to leadership is how to balance divine and human factors in every task we undertake. This principle applies to all aspects of our lives including family leadership, business affairs, and church membership. On the one hand, Nehemiah prayed and sought God's help because he realized he could not solve the problems he faced in his own strength. On the other hand, he worked hard to do everything he could to prepare himself for the moment when God would open a window into the king's mind and heart.

Principle 1

At times we may not be as effective as possible because we don't do all we can to prepare ourselves for our tasks and potential opportunities.

Nehemiah not only prayed and sought God's help concerning the walls and gates of Jerusalem, but he also used all of the human resources available to him. He drew on his intellectual skills, his human experiences, his accumulated wisdom, his role and position, and the people with whom he came in contact.

Nehemiah did his homework. By the time the king asked him what his request was, Nehemiah knew he needed a significant leave of absence, a handful of travel permits, and a blank check to purchase building supplies for walls, gates, the temple complex, and his private home. He was smart enough to ask for all this without identifying Jerusalem by name, since Jerusalem had a history of rebellion. He made his appeal for his ancestral home, knowing that all Middle Easterners honored their ancestors. Nehemiah teaches us that relying on prayer alone is never God's way of achieving His goals on earth. Merely trusting Him as the Sovereign of the universe is a very superficial theological approach. God is indeed sovereign, but He has placed on all of us significant human responsibilities.

True, it is sometimes difficult to balance these two seemingly distinct thrusts pragmatically. However, it is essential that we work at maintaining this balance in order to be effective. Nehemiah is a classic example of striking the balance between prayer and preparation.

AT TIMES, WE MAY NOT BE AS EFFECTIVE AS WE SHOULD BE
BECAUSE WE ARE TRYING TO DO EVERYTHING IN OUR OWN
STRENGTH, WITHOUT THE BALANCE BETWEEN PRAYER AND
PREPARATION.

This principle represents the other extreme—the "peril of the
pendulum"! There are times when we fail as husbands, as fathers, as
businessmen, and as churchmen because we take matters into our own
hands. We don't seek God's help. We rely solely on our own human
wisdom and skills.

True, we may use the words prayer and faith, but they are merely
that—just "words." We are saying the right thing, but still attempting to
solve problems more humanly than spiritually.

It's not easy to maintain this balance between seeking divine favor
and using natural resources. It is a constant challenge, and it's easy to go to
extremes. Nehemiah's example can help us keep our balance by focusing
on praying persistently *and* preparing diligently.

QUESTIONS FOR INTERACTION

1. Most of us are "people of the pendulum" who swing to one extreme or
    the other. When you face a crisis, do you tend to rely on God alone or
    do you tend to rely on yourself alone? Why do you think that is?

2. What is wrong with expecting God to fix your problems apart from
    any effort on your part?

3. What is wrong with trying to solve your problems apart from God?

4. How did Nehemiah demonstrate his dependence on God as he faced
    the overwhelming problem of Jerusalem's defenselessness (1:4-11;
    2:4b)?

5. How did Nehemiah demonstrate that he had been actively planning
    how he could do something about Jerusalem's problems (2:3,5-8)?

6. What kind of risks did Nehemiah take in seizing the opportunity to
    appeal to Artaxerxes for permission to go to Jerusalem and rebuild its
    walls and gates (2:1-4)?

LESSON 2

7. What are the advantages of praying more, as Nehemiah did, before you tackle major problems?

8. How might more prayer affect your courage to put into action the plans you make to handle problems?

GOING DEEPER

9. When you face a problem, do you find it harder to understand the situation itself or the people involved? Give an example.

10. How should your response to question 9 affect the way you pray for God's direction and help? How should it affect the way you research a problem and ask for advice?

11. Nehemiah believed "the God of heaven" ultimately controlled the emperor of Persia. What circumstances, people, or powers do we need to remind ourselves that God controls today?

 ## CARING TIME

We all need support and help in learning to balance the divine and human factors in our lives. We cannot lie back and expect God to do everything for us, and neither can we try to do everything in our own strength and ability. Day by day and week by week, we need to work at avoiding the extremes, and practice living for God in a balanced manner. It's essential that we rely on God for direction and power while at the same time using all the gifts and abilities with which He has blessed us.

1. What has helped you learn to rely on God for guidance and power to face your problems?

2. Choose one problem and share ideas about how to plan a balanced solution, using both reliance on God and human resources.

3. Continue praying for problems that group members identified in the Caring Time of Lesson 1. Have new group members share problems they are facing. Conclude with each man praying for the guy to his left this week.

NEXT WEEK

Next week we will continue exploring the theme of balancing divine and human factors in handling problems. The scene shifts from Susa in Persia to Jerusalem. The problem shifts from seeking permission from the emperor to motivating a discouraged populace. However, the fundamental truth remains the same. The best solution will not happen unless God is behind it, and nothing will happen if people don't play out the roles God gives them in the process. We have seen Nehemiah at prayer and facing a VIP. Next week we meet Nehemiah the strategist and motivator.

SCRIPTURE NOTES

NEHEMIAH 2:1-8

2:1 month of Nisan in the twentieth year. March–April 444 or 445 B.C., some four months after Nehemiah received the report from Hanani about Jerusalem (1:1).

never been sad in his presence. Servants were expected to be dignified and invisible. Nehemiah committed a serious breach of court etiquette when he allowed his distress to show. He may have done it on purpose to provoke a response from Artaxerxes.

2:2 overwhelmed with fear. If Nehemiah's visible distress was unintentional, his terror came from the possibility of offending the king. If he had intentionally displayed his feelings, his terror arose from the realization that he had but a moment in which to say and do exactly the right thing to achieve his goal.

2:3 May the king live forever! A servant was never to display negative emotions in front of the king lest they be interpreted as dissatisfaction or criticism of the king. A servant's job and life could be jeopardized as a result. Yet Artaxerxes noticed Nehemiah's expression and inquired. Although afraid, Nehemiah boldly answered the king.

2:4 So I prayed. Nehemiah had prepared himself for this opportunity by prayer and fasting. He made his final plea for success to God and courteously revealed the desire of his heart to the king.

to the God of heaven. The Jews who grew up in captivity in Babylon developed a theology that recognized the Lord's control of all the nations and empires of the earth. He is more than the God who blesses His people in the land of Canaan. "God of heaven" became a post-exile phrase for His worldwide sovereignty (2 Chron. 36:23; Ezra 1:2; 5:11-12; 6:9-10; 7:12,21,23; Neh. 1:5; 2:4,20; Dan. 2:18-19,37,44).

2:6 the queen seated beside him. The presence of the queen complicated Nehemiah's task. He had to be diplomatic about asking Artaxerxes to reverse his opposition to the rebuilding of Jerusalem. He did not want to make the king look indecisive in front of the queen. Interestingly, the Septuagint (Greek Old Testament) and the Vulgate (Latin Bible) both imply the queen joined her husband in talking sympathetically to Nehemiah about his proposed journey to Jerusalem.

How long will your journey take? Nehemiah probably asked for a short leave of absence. As it turned out, he was away at least 12 years (Neh. 5:14). He most likely had to ask for several extensions as time passed.

PERSONAL NOTES

BUILDING UP YOUR CREW

LAST WEEK

In last week's lesson, we saw Nehemiah seize a crucial opportunity to advance his dream project of rebuilding the defensive walls and gates of Jerusalem. He knew he had a small window of opportunity and he took it. He had prepared himself to be perceptive by praying and seeking God's will in a disciplined manner for four months. As he prayed, plans had formed in his mind. The plans were products of his praying and of his experience in government. Both God and Nehemiah devised the plans. Then Nehemiah dared to approach the king and ask for permission to rebuild Jerusalem, and God moved the king to grant his request. Divine initiative and human initiative go hand-in-hand to accomplish God's will.

ICEBREAKER

For the first three days after Nehemiah arrived in Jerusalem, he kept what he was doing under wraps. He needed to know the situation better before making his plans public. Who knows what the people of Jerusalem thought of this stranger who showed up with Persian infantry and cavalry in tow. He said and did nothing—or so it seemed. Curiosity must have eaten them alive. There is nothing like a secret to drive people nuts.

1. When you were a boy, what was the biggest secret you ever had to keep? How hard was it for you to keep that secret?

2. What is the biggest secret anyone ever kept from you? How did you find out about it?

3. Who in your family is best at keeping birthday or holiday surprises secret? Do you enjoy those surprises? Why or why not?

BIBLICAL FOUNDATION

Nehemiah had experienced an incredible miracle (Neh. 2:7-9). King Artaxerxes had given him beyond what he'd asked for. In addition to safe-passage letters and authorization to requisition building materials from the king's forest, Artaxerxes sent Nehemiah off with a full military escort. Can you imagine the excitement that must have gripped Nehemiah's heart? After months of praying, mourning, and fasting at the prospect of an impossible task, he found himself square in the middle of the king's escort headed for Jerusalem.

Nehemiah knew that what lay before him was daunting. For 150 years, the Jews had been trying to restore Jerusalem with little success. Local leaders opposed a strong Jerusalem. Persian policy had vacillated regarding the Jewish capital city. Nehemiah believed God had brought him to this moment in Israel's history to do a great work. He had experienced too many miracles to begin to doubt now.

God's Strength Through Nehemiah's Strength

⁹ I went to the governors of the region west of the Euphrates and gave them the king's letters. The king had also sent officers of the infantry and cavalry with me. ¹⁰ When Sanballat the Horonite and Tobiah the Ammonite official heard that someone had come to seek the well-being of the Israelites, they were greatly displeased. *(See map in Lesson 4 ...)*

¹¹ After I arrived in Jerusalem and had been there three days, ¹² I got up at night and [took] a few men with me. I didn't tell anyone what my God had laid on my heart to do for Jerusalem. The only animal I took was the one I was riding. ¹³ I went out at night through the Valley Gate toward the Serpent's Well and the Dung Gate, and I inspected the walls of Jerusalem that had been broken down and its gates that had been destroyed by fire. ¹⁴ I went on to the Fountain Gate and the King's Pool, but farther down it became too narrow for my animal to go through. ¹⁵ So I went up at night by way of the valley and inspected the wall. Then heading back, I entered through the Valley Gate and returned. ¹⁶ The officials did not know where I had gone or what I was doing, for I had not yet told the Jews, priests, nobles, officials, or the rest of those who would be doing the work. ¹⁷ So I said to them, "You see the trouble we are in. Jerusalem lies in ruins and its gates have been burned down. Come, let's rebuild Jerusalem's wall, so that we will no longer be a disgrace." ¹⁸ I told them how the gracious hand of my God had been on me, and what the king had said to me.

They said, "Let's start rebuilding," and they were encouraged to [do] this good work.

¹⁹ When Sanballat the Horonite, Tobiah the Ammonite official, and Geshem the Arab heard [about this], they mocked and despised us, and said, "What is this you're doing? Are you rebelling against the king?"

²⁰ I gave them this reply, "The God of heaven is the One who will grant us success. We, His servants, will start building, but you have no share, right, or historic claim in Jerusalem."

Nehemiah 2:9-20

Principles to Live By

There is a saying that there are three kinds of people in the world—those who watch what's happening, those who know what's happening, and those who make things happen. Nehemiah was the third kind of person. He made things happen.

However, when Nehemiah made things happen, it wasn't just because of his ingenuity and hard work. Nehemiah's success depended on God's blessing that was blended with human diligence. Nehemiah understood this truth. When King Artaxerxes gave him letters authorizing him to cross borders and requisition materials from the king's forest outside Jerusalem, Nehemiah said, "The king granted my requests, for I was graciously strengthened by my God" (Neh. 2:8).

Principle 1

WE MUST CONTINUE STRIVING TO MAINTAIN A PROPER BALANCE BETWEEN RELYING ON GOD AND EXERTING HUMAN EFFORTS AS WE CARRY OUT OUR GOD-GIVEN RESPONSIBILITIES.

Nehemiah had prepared himself thoroughly for the moment when Artaxerxes asked him about his dejected countenance. He had well-thought-out answers on the tip of his tongue. Even when he was responding to Artaxerxes' additional questions, he was quietly praying for divine guidance in order to respond wisely.

The same thing happened in Nehemiah's life once he arrived in Jerusalem. If he was going to convince the children of Israel that they should start rebuilding, he knew he needed to thoroughly prepare a strategy in advance and then carefully, but confidently, unveil that plan with discretion and wisdom.

And yet, Nehemiah also knew that an ingenious plan alone would not turn the tide. He had to convince the children of Israel that God would help them accomplish this task. To get this point across, he shared with them his own experience with Artaxerxes several months before.

We must continually exert conscious effort to maintain a proper balance between relying upon God and using our own human talents and abilities. Maintaining this balance in itself calls for "human effort." It does not happen automatically. God places a significant amount of responsibility on us. In this sense, the scale that so delicately balances God's sovereignty and human responsibility tips in our direction. We are responsible to take this initiative.

Nehemiah faced more than toppled walls and burnt gates. He had to deal with people who were demoralized. For 150 years, the population of Judah and Jerusalem had failed in every effort to secure the city's defenses. For 150 years, the leaders of neighboring provinces had successfully opposed every Jewish effort to lift Jerusalem from its rubble.

It took Nehemiah at least two months to travel from Susa to Jerusalem, but it did not take news of his coming long to reach Jerusalem. The Jews must have groaned at the thought of another hotshot who would put them through another cycle of hope and frustration. Their local enemies most likely huddled together to figure out how to honor the newcomer's permits while undermining his efforts.

Nehemiah had to overcome inertia, negative thinking, and impending divisions among God's people. He also had to prepare for the effects of outside opposition. There was no way Nehemiah could accomplish all that on his own. He had to plead with God to intervene on behalf of His chosen people.

On the other hand, Nehemiah had to use all of his considerable leadership skills and broad experience in court intrigues to motivate the Jews and anticipate the plots of their opponents. He quietly and quickly surveyed the situation on the ground and roughed out a plan to secure the city more rapidly than anyone could have imagined. He summoned the people of Jerusalem and hit the problem head on. He challenged them to build. To give them confidence, he reported how God had already helped him miraculously in gaining imperial approval and resources for the entire project. At some point during his report, negative feelings turned positive. Despair turned to hope. They believed Nehemiah and joined together enthusiastically behind the rebuilding project.

The unity of God's people is a theological reality. In God's mind, we are one because we have put our faith in Jesus Christ as our Lord and Savior. However, we must apply this doctrinal truth before it can become a practical truth in our lives. Today's churches—like the churches of the New Testament—are full of people who are, theologically speaking, one in Christ but who, practically speaking, do not get along.

God has taken the initiative to make us one by sending His Son to die on the cross to destroy every barrier separating us from Him and from one another. The responsibility is ours to apply that amazing truth about unity. Practical and visible unity in the church will happen only when we who bear the name of Jesus accept that responsibility. We must do what it takes to love one another, forgive one another, and bear one another's burdens.

QUESTIONS FOR INTERACTION

1. When you start a new job, how do you go about getting familiar with the company and your fellow workers?

2. What have you found to be the biggest rookie mistakes a new person on a job can make?

3. How did Nehemiah approach the area leaders whom he knew were hostile to the idea of a strong Jerusalem (vv. 9-10, 19-20)?

4. How did Nehemiah initially approach the leaders of Jerusalem whom he knew were fearful that they would never be able to secure the city (vv. 11-12, 16)?

5. What was Nehemiah doing during the three days that he kept to himself (vv. 12-15)?

6. How did Nehemiah encourage and motivate the discouraged Jews (vv. 17-18)?

7. How did Nehemiah display his reliance on God in this situation (vv. 18, 20)? How did he accept the responsibility of using his gifts and abilities for God's work?

8. What gifts and abilities do you think God especially expects you to use in His service? How can you use them with greater responsibility?

GOING DEEPER

9. Which of the following best describes how you react to a challenge that will lead to either great success or great failure?
   a. I tend to fixate on the likelihood of failure and worry myself sick.
   b. That kind of challenge energizes me and brings out the best in me.
   c. I do my best and let the chips fall where they may.

10. Based on the response you made to question 9, how should you rely on God in this kind of challenge? For what kinds of help should you and our group be praying?

11. How much do you think an extended investment in prayer, such as Nehemiah made in chapter 1, would help you in knowing the will of God and in making good plans for this kind of threatening challenge?

Caring Time

It's important that we have absolute confidence in God's sovereign control of our lives and total commitment to doing our best to serve Him faithfully. We have to learn to balance our practical belief in the sovereignty of our God with our responsibility to carry out His will.

1. What Scriptures give you certainty that God is in control of your life? What experiences have confirmed this to you?

2. What Scriptures challenge you to accept responsibility to work hard to please God? What experiences have confirmed the importance of taking responsibility for jobs that God gives you to do?

3. Share with the man next to you how you would like to grow in your ability to balance confidence in God's sovereignty with commitment to accept your responsibilities. Pray aloud for the man who shared his request with you.

Next Week

Next week we will look at how Nehemiah organized the people of Jerusalem and Judah to rebuild rapidly the walls and gates of Jerusalem. At first glance, Nehemiah 3 looks like one of those Scripture portions we would rather skip over in order to pick up the flow of the story on the other side. It is full of obscure names of people and unknown places. These names and places meant something to the people who were there, but we doubt this can have any significance nearly 2500 years later. Nevertheless, it does. Nehemiah 3 shows the genius of Nehemiah in getting the maximum effort from his workers while giving them the maximum sense of accomplishment. He built walls and morale at the same time.

Scripture Notes

Nehemiah 2:9-20

2:9 governors of the region west of the Euphrates. Persia organized its empire into twenty or more satrapies. One satrapy covered "the region west of the Euphrates" or Syria. Judah did not have official status as a province of this satrapy. Persia associated Judah with the province of Samaria.

2:10 Sanballat . . . and Tobiah. Sanballat was or would soon become governor of Samaria to the north of Jerusalem. Tobiah is a Jewish name meaning, "The Lord is good." He probably was a worldly Jew controlling the territory east of the Jordan River that had historically belonged to Ammon. Sanballat and Tobiah became Nehemiah's two chief opponents.

2:11 had been there three days. He prepared himself with prayer, thought, and research before trusting a few men with his plans.

2:13 inspected the walls of Jerusalem. Nehemiah surveyed the walls at night, no doubt to make plans before he let others know his intentions. He traveled clockwise along the southern and eastern walls where the terrain was steepest and the rebuilding would be the most difficult. It is hard to tell whether he inspected the entire wall or turned back when piles of rubble made the route impassable.

2:14 too narrow for my animal. Along the southeast wall, the hillside was too steep and the rubble too jumbled for Nehemiah's mount. He either continued on foot or turned back.

2:15 entered through the Valley Gate and returned. This was Nehemiah's starting point in the southwest wall, traveling through the gate into the Hinnon Valley.

2:17 Jerusalem lies in ruins. Nebuchadnezzar had destroyed the walls and gates in 586 B.C. Although attempts had been made to repair them, the work had not been completed.

2:18 gracious hand of my God. Nehemiah combined challenge with encouragement. He urged the people to rebuild the wall, noting the disgrace and trouble resulting from its ruin. He reminded them that God would enable the work in the same way He had given Nehemiah favor with King Artaxerxes.

2:19 Geshem the Arab. Geshem led a confederation of Arab tribes that controlled the deserts south of Judah. Together the territory of Sanballat (north), Tobiah (east), and Geshem (south) completely hemmed in Judah against the Mediterranean Sea to the west.

PERSONAL NOTES

Constructing a Vision of Hope

Last Week

Last week we saw Nehemiah move from the splendor of the Persian capital, Susa, to the obscurity of the Jewish capital, Jerusalem. He had seized a window of opportunity to get permission from King Artaxerxes to come to Jerusalem and rebuild its walls. Once there, he had to create another window of opportunity in which he could motivate the residents of Jerusalem to shake off their discouragement and dare to rise up and rebuild. We saw last week how Nehemiah worked nonstop for three days to size up the situation in Jerusalem and devise a plan. Then he challenged the assembled populace to build, encouraging them with stories about how God had miraculously worked through Artaxerxes to get the project approved, funded, and supplied.

Icebreaker

Many men like to build things. We may not build a city wall, but we still feel like we have accomplished something when a project is successfully completed. Occasionally, we may have to redefine our building success. In an early comedy album, Bill Cosby told about his high school shop class. He said that no matter what project he worked on, he eventually cut two grooves in it and called it an ashtray!

1. When you were growing up, what was the best thing you ever built?
   a. A model airplane, car, or boat
   b. A birdhouse
   c. A jigsaw puzzle
   d. A tree fort
   e. A car engine
   f. Other _____

2. As an adult, what is the most disastrous home repair project you have survived?

3. Which of these are you best at constructing? Give an example.
   a. A building
   b. An organizational plan
   c. An artistic creation

d. A team of people to do a job

e. A schematic diagram

f. Other _____

BIBLICAL FOUNDATION

Like a number of Old Testament passages, Nehemiah 3 is packed with names that are hard to pronounce, information that seems unusually redundant, and chronology that appears meaningless to us today. It was very relevant, however, to the people of Jerusalem.

What we see in this chapter are the job assignments that resulted from Nehemiah's nighttime survey of Jerusalem's walls. Nehemiah 3 reflects an ingenious plan that sprang from our hero's incredible leadership skills.

To understand this chapter it is helpful to look at a map of fifth-century Jerusalem. Locate the Sheep Gate just north of the temple area, and follow the wall from gate to gate in a counterclockwise direction as you read about where various people built. Scholars are uncertain about how much of Nehemiah's new wall encompassed the city that Babylon destroyed. It is likely that much of the southwest part of the city that Hezekiah had annexed (2 Chron. 32:5) was left outside because of a greatly reduced population (Neh. 11:1-2). The list of workers for the southwestern portion of the wall (vv. 9-14) suggests a greatly reduced circuit.

Nehemiah's Jerusalem

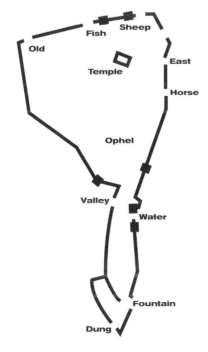

Workers of Jerusalem, Unite!

[1] Eliashib the high priest and his fellow priests began rebuilding the Sheep Gate. They dedicated it and installed its doors. [After building the wall] to the Tower of the Hundred and the Tower of Hananel, they dedicated it. [2] The men of Jericho built next to Eliashib, and next to them Zaccur son of Imri built.

[3] The sons of Hassenaah built the Fish Gate. They built it with beams and installed its doors, bolts, and bars. [4] Next to them Meremoth son of Uriah, son of Hakkoz, made repairs. Beside them Meshullam son of Berechiah, son of Meshezabel, made repairs. Next to them Zadok son of Baana made repairs. [5] Beside them the Tekoites made repairs, but their nobles did not lift a finger to help their supervisors.

[6] Joiada son of Paseah and Meshullam son of Besodeiah repaired the Old Gate. They built it with beams and installed its doors, bolts, and bars. [7] Next to them Melatiah the Gibeonite, Jadon the Meronothite, and the men of Gibeon and Mizpah, who were under the authority of the governor of the region west of the Euphrates River. [8] After him Uzziel son of Harhaiah, the goldsmith, made repairs, and next to him Hananiah son of the perfumer made repairs. They restored Jerusalem as far as the Broad Wall.

[9] Next to them Rephaiah son of Hur, ruler over half the district of Jerusalem, made repairs. [10] After them Jedaiah son of Harumaph made repairs across from his house. Next to him Hattush the son of Hashabneiah made repairs. [11] Malchijah son of Harim and Hasshub son of Pahath-moab made repairs to another section, as well as to the Tower of the Ovens. [12] Beside him Shallum son of Hallohesh, ruler over half the district of Jerusalem, made repairs—he and his daughters.

[13] Hanun and the inhabitants of Zanoah repaired the Valley Gate. They rebuilt it and installed its doors, bolts, and bars, and repaired 500 yards of the wall to the Dung Gate. [14] Malchijah son of Rechab, ruler over the district of Beth-haccerem, repaired the Dung Gate. He rebuilt it and installed its doors, bolts, and bars.

[15] Shallun son of Col-hozeh, ruler over the district of Mizpah, repaired the Fountain Gate. He rebuilt it and roofed it. Then he installed its doors, bolts, and bars. He also made repairs to the wall of the Pool of Shelah near the king's garden, as far as the stairs that descend from the city of David.

[16] After him Nehemiah son of Azbuk, ruler over half the district of Beth-zur, made repairs up to [a point] opposite the tombs of David, as far as the artificial pool and the House of the Warriors. [17] Next to him the Levites made repairs [under] Rehum son of Bani. Beside him Hashabiah,

ruler over half the district of Keilah, made repairs for his district. [18] After him their fellow [Levites] made repairs [under] Binnui son of Henadad, ruler over half the district of Keilah. [19] Next to him Ezer son of Jeshua, ruler over Mizpah, made repairs to another section opposite the ascent to the armory at the Angle.

[20] After him Baruch son of Zabbai diligently repaired another section, from the Angle to the door of the house of Eliashib the high priest. [21] Beside him Meremoth son of Uriah, son of Hakkoz, made repairs to another section, from the door of Eliashib's house to the end of his house. [22] And next to him the priests from the surrounding area made repairs.

[23] After them Benjamin and Hasshub made repairs opposite their house. Beside them Azariah son of Maaseiah, son of Ananiah, made repairs beside his house. [24] After him Binnui son of Henadad made repairs to another section, from the house of Azariah to the Angle and the corner. [25] Palal son of Uzai [made repairs] opposite the Angle and tower that juts out from the upper palace of the king, by the courtyard of the guard. Beside him Pedaiah son of Parosh, [26] and the temple servants living on Ophel [made repairs] opposite the Water Gate toward the east and the tower that juts out. [27] Next to him the Tekoites made repairs to another section from [a point] opposite the great tower that juts out, as far as the wall of Ophel.

[28] Each of the priests made repairs above the Horse Gate, each opposite his own house. [29] After them Zadok son of Immer made repairs opposite his house. And beside him Shemaiah son of Shecaniah, guard of the East Gate, made repairs. [30] Next to him Hananiah son of Shelemiah and Hanun the sixth son of Zalaph made repairs to another section.

After them Meshullam son of Berechiah made repairs opposite his room. [31] Next to him Malchijah, one of the goldsmiths, made repairs to the house of the temple servants and the merchants, opposite the Inspection Gate, and as far as the upper room of the corner. [32] The goldsmiths and merchants made repairs between the upper room of the corner and the Sheep Gate.

Nehemiah 3:1-32

PRINCIPLES TO LIVE BY

Cyril Barber in his book, *Nehemiah and the Dynamics of Effective Leadership* (Christian Focus Publications, 2004), identifies the following key principles that made Nehemiah such a great leader and an outstanding role model for today's key leaders in churches, businesses, government and educational institutions.

PRINCIPLE 1

THE PRINCIPLE OF COORDINATION: TO WHAT EXTENT DO YOU "PLAN YOUR WORK" AND THEN "WORK YOUR PLAN"?

Nehemiah had a phenomenal ability to coordinate people and get everyone involved. This didn't just happen. It *never* "just happens." What appears to be a smooth-running operation always reflects a lot of careful, behind-the-scenes planning.

Neither was the distribution of laborers around the walls of Jerusalem the result of a spontaneous movement of God's Spirit that suddenly put every man and woman in a particular place around the wall, doing a specific job. Rather, Nehemiah spent hours and hours doing careful research, analyzing the data, and putting his plan together.

Remember too that once people were in their assigned places, they needed careful supervision. They also needed adequate resources. Nehemiah thought through all of these things ahead of time.

Effective planning is essential, no matter what our vocation in life. Every task that is done well requires careful forethought.

Good planning begins on paper, but it must not remain there. It's one thing to write our goals—it's another to achieve these goals. It's one thing to have a job description—it is yet another to translate these responsibilities and ideas into action. Still, we must never forget the spiritual aspect of planning. To be truly successful, we need to balance our efforts with prayer and faith in God.

PRINCIPLE 2

THE PRINCIPLE OF COOPERATION: TO WHAT EXTENT ARE YOU UTILIZING YOUR GIFTS, YOUR ABILITIES, AND YOUR PERSONAL RESOURCES TO BUILD UP THE PEOPLE OF GOD?

Perhaps Nehemiah's greatest achievement was gaining the cooperation of a large, diverse building force over the entire life of the project. He assigned most of the workers from Jerusalem to sections of the wall near their residences. These builders were motivated to do good work to protect their families and property. Some workers, such as the priests, built near their places of employment. Workers from neighboring communities worked on stretches of the wall away from the homes of Jerusalem builders.

Nehemiah employed various political leaders as overseers of segments of the wall reconstruction. These men were established leaders with the respect of their communities. Nehemiah succeeded in getting all of these leaders to cooperate wholeheartedly.

In the church of Jesus Christ, God expects us to cooperate. He compares the church to a "body" (1 Cor. 12:12-27), "a spiritual house" (1 Pet. 2:5), and His "household" (Eph. 2:19). In all of these metaphors, every member must contribute his or her efforts for the well-being of the group.

God's plan is clear. He wants every Christian to participate in building the church. He needs everyone to get involved. "We who are many are one body in Christ and individually members of one another" (Rom. 12:5).

PRINCIPLE 3

THE PRINCIPLE OF COMMENDATION: TO WHAT EXTENT ARE YOU AN ENCOURAGER, A REAL PEOPLE PERSON?

Nehemiah was also an encourager. In chapter 3 alone, he mentioned 75 people by name and, in many instances, recognized their accomplishments. He also mentioned at least 15 *groups* of people, such as the priests, Levites, the goldsmiths, the perfumers, and the temple servants. He also identified a number of groups from other towns and cities.

Nehemiah definitely worked to be a "people person." He not only knew these people by name, but where they worked on the wall and what they accomplished. This took time and effort. We can certainly agree that this paid rich dividends when it came to motivating these people to do their best.

At this point, we can take a lesson from Paul. As he concluded his letter to the Romans, he greeted no less than 26 people by name, commending them for their dedication to Christ and their ministry accomplishments. Perhaps Paul learned how important this was from Nehemiah!

Christians, of all people, should encourage each other. If we don't, we are directly disobeying specific commands of Scripture. "Therefore *encourage one another* and build each other up," wrote Paul to the

Thessalonians (1 Thess. 5:11). We also read in the Book of Hebrews, "And let us be concerned about one another in order to promote love and good works, not staying away from our meetings, as some habitually do, but *encouraging each other*, and all the more as you see the day drawing near" (Heb. 10:24-25).

QUESTIONS FOR INTERACTION

1. When you think about becoming an organized leader, which of the following statements best describes how you react?
    a. Great! I love organization.
    b. Good. I need to work on improving my organizational skills.
    c. Oh, okay. I don't want to, but I need to.
    d. Sorry. That just ain't gonna happen.

2. What did Nehemiah gain by involving so many people in rebuilding the wall of Jerusalem? What are the challenges that come along with a large workforce?

3. What were the benefits of assigning some groups to build near their homes (vv. 10, 23, 28-30)?

4. What advantages were there to assigning some workers by occupational groupings (vv. 1, 8, 17-18, 22, 26, 32)?

5. Why would people from surrounding towns and villages want to help fortify Jerusalem (vv. 2, 5, 7, 13)?

6. Why would Nehemiah give special credit to the district leaders who supervised construction (vv. 9, 12, 14-19)?

7. What might Baruch have done to get an "atta boy" for diligence (v. 20)? What does it say about Nehemiah as a leader that he called special attention to Baruch?

8. When you look at the scope of Nehemiah's plan for rebuilding the wall, what impresses you most? How would you like this leadership quality to express itself in your life?

GOING DEEPER

9. How do you plan your day's work? How do you determine if you have successfully worked your plan for the day?

10. In what ways are you involved in the life of your church so that your gifts and abilities benefit the whole body of Christ?

11. How do you encourage people? How could you become a better encourager?

CARING TIME

A challenge to become a more organized leader is a double-edged sword. Nehemiah's example may invigorate us like a tonic and motivate us to excel. On the other hand, his achievement may strike us as an unobtainable standard that leaves us overwhelmed with guilt. God is not looking for clones of Nehemiah. He gave us this account so we would know about His marvelous work for His people through this man. What we apply to our situations from Nehemiah's example will depend on how God is shaping our individual lives.

1. What do you admire about Nehemiah's leadership? Does he intimidate you in any way? If so, how?

2. As you go into this next week, will you be working on better coordination, better cooperation, or better commendation? What will you do about it?

3. Pray for one other man in the group that he will grow in the leadership skill he wants to work on in the coming week.

NEXT WEEK

Next week we will begin looking at some of the problems that arose during the building project and how Nehemiah handled them. Several of the remaining lessons deal with opposition from outside and conflict within the people of God. That shouldn't surprise us, but it shouldn't discourage us either. Nehemiah can teach us many important lessons about trusting God, working as a team, and showing personal courage in the face of opposition. Next week we will look at some of the schemes the Evil One uses to discourage us.

Scripture Notes

Nehemiah 3:1-32

3:1 Eliashib the high priest and his fellow priests. A grandson of Jeshua, the high priest in Zerubbabel's day (Ezra 3:2). He and the other priests, as leaders of the people, started rebuilding the city walls.

rebuilding the Sheep Gate. This gate was used to bring sheep to the temple for sacrifice. It was on the city's northeast side, just north of the temple.

Tower of the Hundred and the Tower of Hananel. Located between the Sheep Gate and the Fish Gate, the towers protected the city's northern approaches.

3:3 built the Fish Gate. Perhaps the gate through which people of Tyre brought fish to market. It may have been located near the site of the modern Damascus Gate.

3:5 the Tekoites. Amos' hometown, about 12 miles south of Jerusalem.

but their nobles. These men disdained manual labor and did not help with the work.

3:10 made repairs across from his house. It would seem sensible to have the workers make the repairs closest to their homes. Even the priests were involved in the repairs (v. 28).

3:12 he and his daughters. Several family groups worked on the walls. Shallum's daughters could not have been the only women who toiled to build the walls. They must have performed notable work to receive special mention.

3:15-25 The greatest concentration of workers built the southeastern section of the wall from the Dung Gate to the Water Gate. The walls of the Kidron Valley were very steep. This is where Nehemiah's mount could not find footing to carry him further (2:14). Archaeologists speculate the workers had to terrace the slope to create and to brace the foundation for the wall.

3:28 Horse Gate. Located in the easternmost part of the city, this gate led to the Kidron Valley. It may have been an entrance for horses coming to the palace area.

PERSONAL NOTES

LESSON 4

DEMOLISHING DISCOURAGEMENT

LAST WEEK

Last week we saw the results of Nehemiah's three-day inspection and planning session after his arrival at Jerusalem. First, he worked out his plan on paper. He sized up the physical needs of the defenseless city. He learned who the willing workers were. He matched up the workers with the parts of the project that would motivate them while they worked. He found out who the leaders were and assigned them key tasks.

Then the hard part came when Nehemiah had to challenge everyone to step into place and start working. In addition, he had to supply everyone with materials and communicate with work crews all around the city walls. In spite of overwhelming responsibility, he did it all in the strength of the Lord whose hand was on him (Neh. 2:18). We came away from last week's lesson challenged to commit ourselves to better organization, to preserving the unity of God's people, and to becoming encouragers of those we lead.

ICEBREAKER

Most of us had to deal with bullies when we were growing up. Maybe the bully you faced was all "talk." Maybe he pushed you around a little. Maybe he beat the snot out of you. Maybe you had a streak of bully in you as you figured out how to get along on the playground and in the neighborhood. Figuring out how to respond to bullies is a big deal in childhood. It can be a big deal in adulthood too.

1. What was your most memorable encounter with a bully when you were a boy? How did you handle it?

2. If you are a father, how have you coached your kids to respond to bullies? If you aren't a father, how would you advise children in a Sunday school class to deal with bullies?

3. Why do you think some bullies are all about threat and intimidation while others actually beat kids up?

LESSON 5

Biblical Foundation

Only reading the first three chapters of Nehemiah might give us the impression that once everyone had been carefully and wisely assigned a particular section of the wall, we could assume that everything progressed smoothly and without difficulty from that point on. Not so! From the moment the reconstruction began, Nehemiah and the Jews faced incredible opposition from their enemies.

God's work *never* goes forward without opposition. Satan sees to that, and Nehemiah's experience in rebuilding the walls of Jerusalem certainly illustrates this point graphically and dramatically.

Round One: Mockery

¹ When Sanballat heard that we were rebuilding the wall, he became furious. He mocked the Jews ² before his colleagues and the powerful men of Samaria, and said, "What are these pathetic Jews doing? Can they restore [it] by themselves? Will they offer sacrifices? Will they ever finish it? Can they bring these burnt stones back to life from the mounds of rubble?" ³ Then Tobiah the Ammonite, who was beside him, said, "Indeed, even if a fox climbed up what they are building, he would break down their stone wall!"

⁴ Listen, our God, for we are despised. Make their insults return on their own heads and let them be taken as plunder to a land of captivity. ⁵ Do not cover their guilt or let their sin be erased from Your sight, because they have provoked the builders.

⁶ So we rebuilt the wall until the entire wall was joined together up to half its [height], for the people had the will to keep working.

Nehemiah 4:1-6

Principles to Live By

Discouragement is one of Satan's most common methods for hindering God's work in our lives. When our morale is low, we are vulnerable to his lies, his slander, and his temptations. For years before Nehemiah arrived in Jerusalem, the Jews in and around the capital city had led a discouraged and demoralized existence. God used Nehemiah to help them rise above their negative circumstances and get on a positive path. His leadership formula can work for us today as well.

PRINCIPLE 1

WE MUST FOCUS AS A **FIRST RESORT** ON PRAYING ABOUT SITUATIONS THAT CAUSE FEAR AND ANXIETY.

At first Sanballat had ignored Nehemiah, seeing him as a mere annoyance. However, he soon realized that Nehemiah had succeeded in elevating Jewish morale and in organizing an effective building campaign. Nehemiah became a threat to Sanballat's power base in Samaria.

Threatened people usually react in one of three ways. They may become extremely fearful and retreat. They may become very angry and aggressive. Or they may blend fear and anger. That is what Sanballat did. Initially he hesitated because of fear. Later he lashed out in anger.

Sanballat engaged in psychological warfare against Israel. He mocked Nehemiah and the Jews (v. 2). In the best "yes-man" fashion, Tobiah joined his boss in the ridicule (v. 3).

Nehemiah reacted to the disheartening sneers of the local bigwigs the same way he had approached every problem so far. He talked earnestly and at length to God about the situation (vv. 4-5). Meanwhile, he persevered stone by stone until "suddenly" the wall had reached half its planned height (v. 6).

God is interested in every detail of our lives, especially our moments of discouragement and disappointment. We all face times when we are anxious and frustrated. During those times, we should pray specifically for encouragement. Often God will answer that prayer by revealing a truth in Scripture or by sending another Christian our way to say or do something that specifically addresses our anxiety or frustration. God wants to provide us the resources to give us His peace—the sense of tranquility and relaxation we need to overcome anxiety when it grips our souls. He does this when we "in everything, through prayer and petition with thanksgiving, let [our] requests be made known to God" (Phil. 4:6).

PRINCIPLE 2

WE MUST BE SURE TO PRAY FOCUSED ON GOD'S WILL, NOT OUR OWN DESIRES, SO THAT WE DON'T CONFUSE OUR OWN DIRECTION WITH HIS. THEN, WE NEED TO READY TO HEAR AND RESPOND TO HIS LEADING.

In Lesson 1, we looked at Nehemiah's initial prayer for Israel, which is a beautiful model for all of us. However, in Nehemiah 4:4-5, we find a prayer we do not want to imitate. Nehemiah prayed that God would bring the tricks of his enemies back on their own heads. He begged God to punish Sanballat and Tobiah harshly for their sins.

Why this prayer? Nehemiah knew that God had already pronounced judgment on the enemies of His covenant people Israel. He knew these enemies had had opportunities to repent, turn to God, and receive forgiveness. (See, for example, Joshua 2:8-13.) Instead, he saw them reject God's grace and choose the path of judgment.

Conversely, Jesus taught us to love our enemies and to pray for them (Matt. 5:43-44). The Apostle Paul forbade us to seek revenge against our enemies. Instead, he urged, "Do not be conquered by evil, but conquer evil with good" (Rom. 12:21). This is God's will for us today in relation to those who oppose His purposes and His people. We should not follow the content of Nehemiah's prayer against his enemies, but we can copy his determination to pray in God's will.

PRINCIPLE 3

WE NEED TO PUT FEET TO OUR PRAYERS BY COMBINING DILIGENT WORK WITH DILIGENT PRAYER.

Some people pray and wait for things to happen, but not Nehemiah! He prayed, and at the same time continued to build the wall (v. 6). He put feet to his prayers. He faced Sanballat's psychological warfare with both spiritual and natural resources. He committed the problem to the Lord and then asked his assistants to "hand him another brick"!

Nehemiah's enthusiasm and confidence in God served as the primary factors that helped the Jews keep their own spirits high. In turn, Israel's positive responses to his leadership enabled Nehemiah to keep his own spirits high. This mutual encouragement was one of God's answers to Nehemiah's prayers.

Sometimes we need to pray before we take action. At other times, we need to pray while we take action. Here are some actions we can take as we pray for protection from discouragement. *(1) Try to avoid both physical and emotional exhaustion.* This only magnifies discouragement. *(2) Be sure to get proper physical exercise.* This is an essential stress-buster. *(3) Spend some time with someone who is not discouraged.* Positive people lift our spirits. Negative people will drag us down. *(4) Do something for someone else.* We need to focus more on others, and less on ourselves. *(5) Accomplish a task.* Do something small to gain some emotional momentum. *(6) Attempt to learn important personal lessons from difficult situations.* God has a purpose for each life. He can give significance to every crisis and disaster as we surrender these situations to Him and walk with Him through them.

1. Which of these statements best describes how you react when you've put a lot of effort into a project and people start criticizing you?
   a. I withdraw in discouragement and self-pity.
   b. I lash out in anger and frustration.
   c. I withdraw some and lash out some.
   d. Other _____.

2. How do you wish you could react when people criticize you while you put your best efforts into what you are doing?

3. What do you think Sanballat and Tobiah hoped to accomplish by mocking the Jews in the presence of their "colleagues and powerful men of Samaria" (v. 2)?

4. What do you think Sanballat and Tobiah hoped would happen when Nehemiah and the Jewish wall builders heard about their mockery?

5. Which of these do you think best captures what was going on in Sanballat and Tobiah's hearts and minds? Why?
   a. Contempt for the loser Jews
   b. Bravado to rally the troops for possible battle
   c. Anxiety about what might happen
   d. Fear that their power was slipping away
   e. Other _____

6. What can we learn positively and negatively from the way Nehemiah prayed about his enemies (vv. 4-5)?

7. How do you think Nehemiah and the builders felt when the wall reached half its projected height in spite of the mockery of their enemies (v. 6)?

8. How do you think God would like you to grow in your ability to stand up under criticism?

GOING DEEPER

9. When you face criticism for doing right, how should you think about your critics?

10. When you face criticism for doing right, how should you pray for your critics?

11. When you face criticism for doing right, what should your attitude be toward the work you are doing?

 ## Caring Time

Nehemiah faced and resisted discouragement that came from opposition to his work. We face discouragement at work too, but discouragement can arise at home, at church, and in other areas of our lives as well. One of the greatest services we can provide for one another in this group is encouragement. Remember, "discouraged" and "disheartened" are synonyms. When we *en*courage one another, we are giving one another courage. We are putting heart back into one another.

1. What discouraging circumstances are you currently dealing with?

2. What have you found through the years to be good sources of encouragement for you?

3. Focus one-by-one on each man in the group and write down two ways you can regularly encourage each other through the balance of this Nehemiah study. Join right now in sharing a few words of encouragement for each man in your group.

Next Week

Next week we will examine the second stage of opposition that Nehemiah and the wall builders encountered from the hands of their opponents. When the surrounding provinces realized they could not intimidate the Jews by mockery, they began to plan a sneak attack to stop the construction before it got much beyond the halfway mark. Since it's difficult to keep an elaborate plot secret, Nehemiah soon learned of it. What would he do? Stop building and call out the National Guard? We'll see.

NEHEMIAH 4:1-6

4:1 Sanballat (later called "governor of Samaria"), he was probably from Beth-Horon, 15 miles northeast of Jerusalem. He may have objected to Nehemiah's return and the reconstruction project because he wanted to gain control of Judah.

4:2 Samaria. The former capital of the northern kingdom of Israel. Samaria had become the capital for the mixed race of people descended from various ethnic groups settled there by the Assyrian empire after it defeated and deported the population of Israel in 722 B.C., some 275 years earlier (2 Kings 17:24-41).

before his colleagues … said. Sanballat was upset when Nehemiah arrived in Jerusalem (2:10). He angrily ridiculed the Jews and accused them of rebelling against the king.

burnt. In his derisive tirade, Sanballat referred to burnt, weakened stones from the old, demolished wall.

4:4 Listen, our God. Nehemiah's consistent pattern was prayer before action. He immediately turned to God in the face of opposition.

PERSONAL NOTES

Renovating Hope

Last Week

In last week's lesson, we reflected on the amazing kickoff of the reconstruction of Jerusalem's walls. We were inspired by the fact that even though all sorts of lies and mockery buzzed through the air around them, "the people had the will to keep working" (Neh. 4:6). This lesson also reminded us how Satan likes to use discouragement to derail God's work in our lives. We noted how important it is to pray about big and small life events to ward off discouragement. We saw the vital necessity of praying in the will of God so we don't confuse our agenda with His. Once again, we saw the connection between praying hard and working hard in the service of God, encouraging one another in the process.

Icebreaker

It's great to hit the locker room at halftime in the lead, secure in the knowledge that momentum is on our side. Momentum, however, can prove to be a fickle teammate. We can't assume that "Mighty Mo" will keep on playing for our team in the second half. Momentum may change uniforms and win the game for the other team.

1. What is your favorite sports movie?
   a. *Rudy*
   b. *The Natural*
   c. *The Mighty Ducks*
   d. *Rocky*
   e. *Hoosiers*
   f. Other _____

2. How does momentum shift back and forth in the movie you selected in question 1?

3. When you were a boy, what was the biggest secret plot you ever helped to pull off?

Since Sanballat's psychological warfare campaign against Nehemiah and the Jews failed miserably, the enemies of the Jews realized they needed a fresh approach to stopping the wall construction … and they needed it immediately! Given the pace of the construction, there was no time to lose. Sanballat and his partners in intrigue hatched a plot to turn the tide of events in their favor.

Round Two: A Conspiracy Theory

[7] When Sanballat, Tobiah, and the Arabs, Ammonites, and Ashdodites heard that the repair to the walls of Jerusalem was progressing and that the gaps were being closed, they became furious. [8] They all plotted together to come and fight against Jerusalem and throw it into confusion. [9] So we prayed to our God and stationed a guard because of them day and night.

[10] In Judah, it was said:

The strength of the laborer fails,
since there is so much rubble.
We will never be able to rebuild the wall.

[11] And our enemies said, "They won't know or see anything until we're among them and can kill them and stop the work." [12] When the Jews who lived nearby arrived, they said to us time and again, "Everywhere you turn, [they] attack us." [13] So I stationed [people] behind the lowest sections of the wall, at the vulnerable areas. I stationed them by families with their swords, spears, and bows. [14] After I made an inspection, I stood up and said to the nobles, the officials, and the rest of the people, "Don't be afraid of them. Remember the great and awe-inspiring Lord, and fight for your countrymen, your sons and daughters, your wives and homes."

[15] When our enemies realized that we knew their scheme and that God had frustrated it, every one of us returned to his own work on the wall.

Nehemiah 4:7-15

PRINCIPLES TO LIVE BY

The Jews were definitely ahead at halftime when they went into the locker room. Nehemiah was clearly a better quarterback. Sanballat, on the other hand, couldn't seem to get his team across the line of scrimmage. When the second half came, things were different. Nehemiah's team had worked their hearts out in the first half. They were physically and emotionally exhausted. That is when Sanballat brought in fresh recruits and a completely new set of plays.

PRINCIPLE 1

IT IS OFTEN MORE DIFFICULT TO COMPLETE THE SECOND HALF OF A TASK THAN THE FIRST HALF, SO WE MUST SEEK STRENGTH FROM GOD TO PRESS ON AND NOT SLUMP BACK.

Nehemiah and the Jewish workers were energized and excited about what they were doing. They had attacked the project with a spirit of unity and zeal to serve the Lord. But once they reached the halfway point in rebuilding the wall around Jerusalem, they faced a normal motivational problem. Even in the best of times, it's easy to let down when you're halfway there. Furthermore, in the face of Sanballat's and Tobiah's mockery, they had used up an incredible amount of emotional and physical energy. As soon as Nehemiah and the people heard that their enemies were plotting a sneak attack from all sides at any moment, physical and psychological fatigue assailed them. As a result, they lost their energy and momentum (4:10).

How many worthy projects in our Christian lives have we tackled enthusiastically only to lose our passion at the halfway point? Remember! It's easy to lose momentum, particularly when we're putting out a lot of energy. It's easy to get caught off guard when we're "winning." It's easy to let down when we grow weary. Satan delights in unfinished tasks, particularly ones that are spiritually productive.

PRINCIPLE 2

BECAUSE FATIGUE COMBINED WITH A SENSE OF UNCERTAINTY MAKES IT DIFFICULT FOR ALL OF US TO EVALUATE REALITY CORRECTLY, WE MUST BECOME PEOPLE OF HOPE.

When Nehemiah and the Jews heard of the secret plot to attack Jerusalem, they met this "corporate threat" with "corporate prayer." Nehemiah's personal prayer model was paying off. He reported, "*We* prayed to *our* God" (v. 9a). They all had learned that prayer and hard work go hand-in-hand. However, their strategy did not yield immediate results. Word kept pouring in of an impending attack (v. 12). Guards were posted at night (v. 9b). Predictably, the task before the children of Israel began to look bigger than it really was. The piles of rubbish seemed to be getting bigger (v. 10).

No matter how bad our personal situations or the problems facing our churches, we must remember that God has called us to be people of hope. As Christians, we should be positive rather than negative people. Nehemiah shows us how to face problems head on. He did not let difficulties overwhelm him, sidetrack him, or defeat him. In God's strength, he rose above the problems of fatigue and uncertainty and succeeded in thwarting his enemies' efforts to destroy him.

Nehemiah had modeled for the Jews both how to pray and how to work hard (v. 9). However, anxiety and fear spawned by daily rumors grew in the hearts of the people. Nehemiah knew he had to keep hope alive. He called both leaders and people together and challenged them to reject fear and trust God. In addition to guards, whole families were put in harm's way to protect the project (v. 13). In view of the threat of annihilation, Nehemiah challenged them to fight for their country, their families, and their homes (v. 14). He would not let a deteriorating situation alter his objectives and his motivation. He would not give up.

Was Nehemiah on a macho ego trip, unable to face inevitable defeat? No. He believed God had led him to Jerusalem to build that wall. He remembered the miraculous way God had moved in the heart of Artaxerxes to authorize and supply the project and believed a completed wall was God's will.

What Nehemiah *was*, the people who followed him were *becoming*. They already prayed like him and worked like him. They listened to him when he called on them to trust the Lord (v. 14). They listened to him when he called on them to fight, no matter what the price.

We all need good models and proper exhortation. Any good leader—whether father, pastor, counselor, or teacher—knows that both are necessary. We must never neglect these qualities in helping others to discover the will of God.

QUESTIONS FOR INTERACTION

1. What circumstances tend to wear you down and keep you from finishing things you start?

2. Does your life situation make you a detailed planner like Nehemiah or a frontline worker like the wall builders? What do you admire about the other kind of person in tough times?

3. What was the plot of the enemies of Nehemiah and Judah (vv. 7-8, 11-12)?

LESSON 6

4. How did news of the conspiracy affect the morale of the workers inside Jerusalem (v. 10)?

5. How did Nehemiah organize a response to the rumor of a surprise attack (vv. 9, 13)?

6. What are the three parts of Nehemiah's challenge to the leaders and people in verse 14? Why is each part important to heading off a surprise attack?

7. Why do you think the enemies all around gave up when the workers prepared to fight them (v. 15)?

8. How can you defend yourself against the lies of Satan when he makes you think he is about to overwhelm you from all sides?

Going Deeper

9. How do you tend to let down as you near the completion of a project? How can you resist these tendencies?

10. As you get tired, how does your perception of reality distort? What clutter or less important things could you remove from your schedule to get more rest and relaxation?

11. How well do you deliver needed exhortation? How well do you receive needed exhortation?

 ## Caring Time

Nehemiah handled the conspiracy against the building project by modeling prayerful courage and by exhorting the workers to stop being afraid, to pray like crazy, and to get ready to fight. In our families, in our work, and in our church responsibilities, we need that kind of courage to be effective leaders during tough times.

1. What worthwhile projects have you started in recent years but left unfinished or at a standstill?

2. Which of these unfinished projects would be spiritually beneficial for your family, your church, or somebody else?

3. What would it take to complete that project? What "tools" would you need? What kind of exhortation or urging would help you? As a leader, what kind of exhortation or urging do you need to give others?

4. Take turns praying for the success of other group members in completing their projects.

Next Week

Next week we'll consider the cold, hard details of the days leading up to the completion of the walls and gates of Jerusalem. The defenses were in place. Workers and leaders had accepted the burden of double duties. It was going to be a long, arduous push to the finish line, but it was too late to back out. In addition, the workers had invested so much in the walls that they wanted to see the job done. Things were as bad as they were going to get. They might as well see it through. They were not forgetting God either. Nehemiah convinced them that they were doing His work.

Scripture Notes

Nehemiah 4:7-15

4:7 *Ammonites.* People east of the Jordan River led by Tobiah. ***Ashdodites.*** Residents of an ancient Philistine city between Judah and the Mediterranean Sea. The people of verse 7 surround Judah: Sanballat to the north, Tobiah and the Ammonites to the east, the Arabs to the south, and the Ashdodites to the west.

4:9 *prayed to our God and stationed a guard.* All those working on the wall joined in Nehemiah's prayer and then prepared to resist the attack.

4:10 *strength of the laborer fails.* Posting a guard did not end the problem. The workers were exhausted, and the job was only half done. Discouragement set in.

4:11 *our enemies said.* The opposition started rumors among the Jews to produce fear and weaken their resolve to complete the task. The rumors contained threats of a secret attack.

4:13 *stationed them by families.* Placing whole families together, including women and children, was dangerous, but Nehemiah knew fathers would fight to protect their families. The Jews had no formal army to defend themselves.

4:14 *Don't be afraid of them. Remember the … Lord.* Nehemiah encouraged the frightened people to remember God's strength and power. The enemies did not attack, and the work on the wall resumed.

FORGING A BAND OF BROTHERS

LAST WEEK

Last week we saw Nehemiah exert his wisdom and strength as a leader. He devised a tactical response to the enemy who plotted to launch a sneak attack at any moment from any direction. He motivated a tiring workforce to take on added responsibility and work longer hours to defend the city while continuing to build the walls. All the while, he urged the people to seek God's protection and assistance. There is, of course, a lesson here for all of us. It's hard not to let down our enthusiasm after experiencing initial success, but if we want to finish well, we need to both work hard and rely on the Lord to the very end.

ICEBREAKER

Most guys love war movies. We admire the courage of William Wallace in *Braveheart*. We feel sorry for Patton who was a military genius but didn't function well off the battlefield. We relish the camaraderie shown in *Band of Brothers* and the dogged determination portrayed in *Saving Private Ryan*. These movies appeal to our competitive nature and our desire to win.

1. When you were a boy, what was your favorite pretend form of fighting?
   a. Cowboys and Indians
   b. War games in the woods
   c. A board game such as *Risk*
   d. A video game such as *Street Fighter*
   e. Wrestling in the backyard
   f. Other _____

2. If your faith were a piece of contemporary military equipment, which of these would it be, and why?
   a. A Kevlar helmet
   b. Night-vision goggles
   c. Heavy-body armor
   d. An NBC suit (nuclear, biological, chemical protection)
   e. An MRE (yummy "meals, ready-to-eat")
   f. An M16 rifle
   g. Other _____

3. What is your favorite war movie, and why?

Biblical Foundation

Nehemiah defeated Sanballat and Tobiah in Round One by maintaining morale in the face of their mockery. He defeated them in Round Two by organizing defenses in anticipation of their surprise attack. To get through the rest of the bout, he had to keep the workforce at a high level of preparation and performance. His leadership was masterful because his faith in God was unshakable.

Gutting It Out

[15] When our enemies realized that we knew their scheme and that God had frustrated it, every one of us returned to his own work on the wall. [16] From that day on, half of my men did the work while the other half held spears, shields, bows, and armor. The officers supported all the people of Judah, [17] who were rebuilding the wall. The laborers who carried the loads worked with one hand and held a weapon with the other. [18] Each of the builders had his sword strapped around his waist while he was building, and the trumpeter was beside me. [19] Then I said to the nobles, the officials, and the rest of the people: "The work is enormous and spread out, and we are separated far from one another along the wall. [20] Wherever you hear the trumpet sound, rally to us there. Our God will fight for us!" [21] So we continued the work, while half of the men were holding spears from daybreak until the stars came out. [22] At that time, I also said to the people, "Let everyone and his servant spend the night inside Jerusalem, so that they can stand guard by night and work by day." [23] And I, my brothers, my men, and the guards with me never took off our clothes. Each carried his weapon, even when washing.

Nehemiah 4:15-23

Principles to Live By

From the time rumors started flying about a sneak attack until the walls and gates were finished took about a month, but that month must have seemed like it would never end. For one thing, the workers didn't know they would finish the walls without being attacked. The grinding fatigue the builders must have experienced during the final couple of weeks is hard to imagine. However, they changed history because a leader and his people got it right. They gave their very best to God and trusted Him to do something miraculous.

WE MUST BE ON CONSTANT GUARD AGAINST OUR GREATEST ENEMY—THE SPIRITUAL FORCES OF EVIL—AND BE READY TO TAKE UP THE FULL ARMOR OF GOD.

When Sanballat and his cohorts discovered that their plan for a secret attack on Jerusalem was common knowledge and the children of Israel had organized to defend themselves, they backed off. From that day on, half of Nehemiah's men "did the work while the other half held spears, shields, bows, and armor" (v. 16). Even those who continued the work carried weapons. Nehemiah also knew the city and its builders were vulnerable due to the dispersion of the workers all around the walls. Consequently, he stationed a trumpeter next to him. In case of an attack, the trumpeter would blow a blast to signal everyone to rush to counterattack the enemy.

Most of our battles as Christians are on a much different level than the one Nehemiah faced. God has not called us to defend our faith with literal weapons. We cannot justify a Christian "holy war" based on God's plan for Israel. As Paul wrote: "For our battle *is not against flesh and blood*, but against the rulers, against the authorities, against the world powers of this darkness, against the *spiritual forces of evil* in the heavens" (Eph. 6:12).

In the following verses, Paul went on to compare a "flesh and blood" battle with our "spiritual" battle. Referring to various pieces of armor and weapons used by various warriors, he made a direct application to our battle against Satan and his host of demons. He urged us to "take up the full armor of God," so that we might defeat Satan (Eph 6:13).

PRINCIPLE 2

WE MUST STAND TOGETHER IN OUR BATTLE AGAINST SATAN IF WE ARE GOING TO WIN. THE ENEMY WORKS TO ISOLATE US.

One of the great challenges Nehemiah faced in rebuilding the wall was to develop a strategy for a unified force in case of attack. "The work is enormous and spread out," he said, "and we are separated far from one another along the wall" (v. 19). As we have seen, he appointed a man who would follow him everywhere he went, and in case of attack he was to sound the trumpet to rally everyone to the spot of battle (v. 20).

Just so, God never intended for Christians to face Satan and his host of demons alone. We need each other. There is strength in unity as well as mutual support and encouragement. Paul addressed his command to put on the armor of God to the church, the spiritual army of God. It isn't a set of instructions for some spiritual Rambo out to take on the devil one-on-one.

Whether we are single men, husbands, fathers, or church leaders,

Satan desires to "break down our walls." He does not want us to come together to build up one another and the church of Jesus Christ. However, as we stand together, armed with the strength of God, we can triumph over Satan and see our homes and churches built up.

Principle 3

WE MUST ACKNOWLEDGE WITH NEHEMIAH THAT, "OUR GOD WILL FIGHT FOR US!" (V. 20).

To make sure the people really knew why they could proceed with confidence, Nehemiah once again underscored the divine nature of their task. In the same breath that he issued a warning to listen for the trumpet blast so they could prepare to take military action, he also promised, "Our God will fight for us!" Once again, Nehemiah was telling the children of Israel that if they did their part, including moving ahead by faith, then God would do His part.

The work went forward. Everyone worked diligently "from daybreak until the stars came out" (v. 21). Those living outside the city didn't even return to their homes. Rather, they spent the night in Jerusalem, laboring by day and guarding by night (v. 22). Even when they stopped to rest, they didn't remove their clothes. They kept their weapons within arms reach so that, at a moment's notice, they could be ready to defend themselves (v. 23).

God expects us to work hard without feeling that our success depends on us. He wants us to put our very best into His hands so He can work through us. Unfortunately, we tend to ignore God and His resources when we are working hard. We only call on Him and rely on Him when we conclude things have gotten too hard for us to handle in our own strength.

It is indeed the Lord's battle. Our lives are His. We serve Him. As we seek His kingdom and His righteousness with all our hearts, He will bless us, strengthen us, and fight alongside us to defeat Satan and his hosts.

QUESTIONS FOR INTERACTION

1. When you are working on a project that is encountering difficulties and looks like it might fall apart, do you tend to feel energized or disheartened, and why?

2. When you face a deteriorating situation, do you think you assess it realistically, too optimistically, or too pessimistically? How does this affect your problem solving?

3. What did each of the following people do during the second half of the wall-building project: the guards, the load carriers, and the builders (vv. 16-18, 21)?

4. What was Nehemiah's warning system in case of an attack and why did it work (vv. 18-20)?

5. What hardships did Nehemiah's security system create for the workers (vv. 21-23)?

6. Why would Nehemiah prepare so conscientiously if he believed that it was God who frustrated his enemies (v. 15) and fought for him (v. 20)?

7. How can we keep from getting discouraged at the prospect of fighting against Satan when he is always out there ready to attack?

8. How can we experience the peace of Christ when we live every day in a spiritual war zone?

GOING DEEPER

9. How much personal effort and discipline do you think it takes to "put on the full armor of God so that all of us together "can stand against the tactics of the Devil" (Eph. 6:11)?

10. What difference does it make in our understanding of the armor of God if we regard it as equipment for individual soldiers who fight alone or equipment for an army that fights as a unit?

11. How can we remind ourselves regularly (as Nehemiah did) that God frustrates our enemy and fights for us in spiritual warfare?

CARING TIME

As noted earlier, Paul told the Ephesians, "Our battle is not against flesh and blood, but against the rulers, against the authorities, against the world powers of this darkness, against the spiritual forces of evil in the heavens" (Eph 6:12). We need to remember that this is *our* collective battle. We are in this together. We miss a tremendous spiritual resource when we go into battle alone. Let us commit ourselves to helping one another—to drawing together as a band of brothers.

1. When you look at the catalog of the armor of God in Ephesians 6:14-17, about which of the pieces of armor would you like further information?

2. Pool and share your group knowledge about the suiting up with pieces of armor identified in your discussion of question 1.

3. How can we call on one another for assistance in battle when we are struggling against Satan and his forces?

Next Week

Next week we will discover that not all of the obstacles to rebuilding the walls of Jerusalem came from outside enemies. Serious internal problems threatened the unity of the Jewish community. Selfishness and greed threatened to do what armies could not—halt the work of God. This turn of events must have devastated Nehemiah, but he knew he had to face the problem and deal with it. It made no sense to fortify Jerusalem if the people inside it were corrupt.

Scripture Notes

Nehemiah 4:15-23

4:17 worked with one hand. Nehemiah armed the workers. Those who carried baskets of rubble on their heads held their weapons in one hand and balanced the baskets with the other. Half the men worked on the wall while the other half stood guard.

4:20 Our God will fight for us! Nehemiah combined faith and effort, trusting God to protect the workers. The trumpeter accompanied Nehemiah as he supervised the work. The trumpet blast served as a battle cry, summoning the people to join forces at the place of attack.

4:21 from daybreak. The workers living outside the city did not return to their homes to sleep. They worked until well after sunset and traveling at night was too dangerous.

4:23 even when washing. The urgency of the project required constant diligence and long, hard hours. The workers toiled night and day, and remained armed at all times.

CEMENTING RELATIONSHIPS IN CONFLICT

LAST WEEK

Last week we watched Nehemiah cope with the unceasing pressures of building the wall while defending against a possible attack by Sanballat and his allies. For the last three or four weeks of the building project, the Jews faced the need to be on guard day and night. In the spiritual realm, we too must continually be on guard against the schemes of Satan. We must stand together as a "band of brothers" in resisting the Evil One. While mustering all our courage and determination to battle evil, we must consistently rely on God as the One who fights for us.

ICEBREAKER

Money causes many problems. (In fairness, it is safe to say it solves quite a few problems too!) We can learn a lot about ourselves by how we manage and use our money, as well as a lot about others by how they use and manage theirs.

1. Which of these statements best describes how you played *Monopoly* as a boy?
   a. I bought everything in sight and won or lost as a big spender.
   b. I went after strategic properties I thought were key to winning.
   c. I teamed up with another player to pick off the others one by one. Then we fought it out.
   d. I usually lost early in the game. I never got the hang of *Monopoly*.
   e. I hated *Monopoly* and seldom played.
   f. Other _____.

2. What was your first paying job? What did you do with the money you earned?

3. How did your parents handle money? How did their example influence you?

Nehemiah's brother, Hanani, had told him when they first met in Susa, "The survivors in the province, who returned from the exile, are in great trouble and disgrace" (Neh. 1:3). Hanani made it clear that more than the walls and gates of Jerusalem needed rebuilding. Ideally, Nehemiah had wanted to complete the physical rebuilding first in the hope that success would inspire the people to seek spiritual renewal as well. As it turned out, some spiritual issues could not wait. These issues needed addressing even as the walls went up.

Rebuilding Social Ethics

[1] There was a widespread outcry from the people and their wives against their Jewish countrymen. [2] Some were saying, "We, our sons, and our daughters are numerous. Let us get grain so that we can eat and live." [3] Others were saying, "We are mortgaging our fields, vineyards, and homes to get grain during the famine." [4] Still others were saying, "We have borrowed money to pay the king's tax on our fields and vineyards. [5] We and our children are [just] like our countrymen and their children, yet we are subjecting our sons and daughters to slavery. Some of our daughters are already enslaved, but we are powerless because our fields and vineyards belong to others." [6] I became extremely angry when I heard their outcry and these complaints. [7] After seriously considering the matter, I accused the nobles and officials, saying to them, "Each of you is charging his countrymen interest." So I called a large assembly against them [8] and said, "We have done our best to buy back our Jewish countrymen who were sold to foreigners, but now you sell your own countrymen, and we have to buy them back." They remained silent and could not say a word. [9] Then I said, "What you are doing isn't right. Shouldn't you walk in the fear of our God [and not invite] the reproach of our foreign enemies? [10] Even I, as well as my brothers and my servants, have been lending them money and grain. Please, let us stop charging this interest. [11] Return their fields, vineyards, olive groves, and houses to them immediately, along with the percentage of the money, grain, new wine, and olive oil that you have been assessing them."

[12] They responded: "We will return [these things] and require nothing more from them. We will do as you say." So I summoned the priests and made everyone take an oath to do this. [13] I also shook the folds of my robe and said, "May God likewise shake from his house and property everyone who doesn't keep this promise. May he be shaken out and have nothing!"

The whole assembly said, " Amen," and they praised the LORD. Then the people did as they had promised.

Nehemiah 5:1-13

LESSON 8

 PRINCIPLES TO LIVE BY

Anyone who's been in a leadership position has had to wrestle with conflict resolution. Some conflicts are easy to resolve. Others are complex and terribly time consuming. Unfortunately, some are unsolvable. Nevertheless, we should face all disagreements squarely and courageously, because internal conflicts must be resolved whenever possible. If they're not, churches will split, families will fall into chaos, and marriages will die.

PRINCIPLE 1

INTERNAL PROBLEMS WITHIN ANY GROUP OF PEOPLE ARE INEVITABLE AND SHOULD BE EXPECTED.

The internal conflict Nehemiah faced in Jerusalem and Judah was so severe it could have scuttled the whole building project. Worse yet, it threatened to bring reproach on the name of the Lord. Some people were running out of food due to focusing their time and energy on the wall project at a time when famine pinched everyone's food supply. Many had mortgaged their homes and land to buy food. Others had borrowed money at exorbitant interest from wealthy fellow Jews. Finally, a wave of foreclosures resulted in the selling of children into slavery to pay their parents' debts.

We can scratch our heads and wonder how such terrible things could happen among God's people. The fact of the matter is there is no perfect group of people—no perfect family, no perfect church, no perfect organization. We are still prone to sin and selfishness, and Satan will see that we have temptation dangling in our faces. Amazingly, many folks really are looking for perfect churches and expecting their families to be perfect.

To be sure, God wills that our internal problems be minimal. But when they arrive, He expects us to solve them. He has given us the resources to defeat Satan's attempts to destroy our human relationships.

PRINCIPLE 2

WE MUST NOT IGNORE INTERNAL CONFLICT; IT DOES NOT HEAL ITSELF.

Can you imagine how Nehemiah must have felt when he faced these new problems? He was already engaged in a psychological battle with Israel's enemies. In addition, he felt the full weight of responsibility for keeping Israel in a state of military preparedness while keeping the wall construction on track.

There are times when a leader wants to give up. The pressures get so great it seems impossible to go on. Surely, Nehemiah had those feelings. Once again, however, we see the power of his character. He had come too far to give up. Morale had hit rock bottom, and he knew he could not show signs of personal fatigue and discouragement.

At the same time, Nehemiah knew he had to act quickly and decisively. Unresolved conflict does not get better by itself. Problems intensify. Interpersonal relationships break down. Open or thinly veiled hostility replaces civility. The life of the family, church, or organization slowly grinds to a halt.

God has given us the resources of His Spirit and His Word to resolve internal conflicts. Two of the most important Scriptures concerning conflict resolution come from Jesus and the Apostle Paul. In Matthew 18:15-17, Jesus tells us how to work within the framework of our church fellowship to restore relationships. In Ephesians 4:25-32, Paul reminds us of the spiritual and emotional qualities we need to exercise in conflict resolution.

PRINCIPLE 3

WE MUST PROPERLY HANDLE THE NEGATIVE EMOTIONS CAUSED BY INTERNAL CONFLICT OR THEY WILL AGGRAVATE THE ISSUES AT HAND.

When Nehemiah heard that Jewish children were being sold into slavery and that wealthy Jews were oppressing poor ones, he "became extremely angry" (v. 6). In spite of his fatigue and stress, low physical and psychological tolerance did not prompt Nehemiah's anger. The selfishness, greed, and insensitivity of some of his fellow Jews caused his fury.

In spite of his intense anger, Nehemiah did not take immediate action. Rather, he backed off, got control of himself, and did some very careful and serious thinking. He established some emotional distance from the problem so he could gain proper perspective.

Internal strife always causes negative emotions, both in the leader and in others. As leaders, we must be prepared to handle these negative emotions constructively and biblically. We need to ask whether we are angry because of personal offense or because a wrong has been done. We need to allow time to clear away some of the emotional fog that interferes with objective thinking. We need to beware of displaying anger in a public setting since there is no quicker way to lose respect.

PRINCIPLE 4

IN SOLVING CONFLICTS AMONG PEOPLE, WE MUST LEAD BY EXAMPLE. OUR CONSISTENT MODEL OF INTEGRITY FORMS THE FOUNDATION FOR EFFECTIVE EXHORTATION AND CONFRONTATION.

Nehemiah pulled no punches when he finally confronted the offending "nobles and officials" (v. 7). He could expose their hypocrisies and inconsistencies because he had a track record of compassion and selfless concern for others. He didn't hesitate to point out what he and others had been doing to help the poor among the Jewish community (vv. 8, 10). He made it clear that he and others had been paying money out of their pockets to free indebted and enslaved Jews.

Nehemiah said, "What you are doing isn't right. Shouldn't you walk in the fear of our God and not invite the reproach of our foreign enemies?" (v. 9). He charged the Jewish oppressors with dishonoring God's name and reputation. He challenged them to change their immoral and unethical behavior. Best of all, he gave them an example to follow.

One of the primary reasons Nehemiah was successful in handling an intense and very difficult situation is that he exemplified with his own life what he asked others to do. This leadership principle applies to all of our relationships as Christians, particularly when we are in a leadership role. For instance, as fathers we must consistently visualize and dramatize for our children the kind of life we want them to live.

QUESTIONS FOR INTERACTION

1. Which of these statements best describes your attitude toward conflict resolution?
   a. Bring it on. I'm good at reconciling people.
   b. It'll give me an ulcer, but I can do it if I have to.
   c. I put off conflict resolution as long as I can.
   d. I've never met a conflict I couldn't duck.
   e. Other _____.

2. How do you tend to react emotionally during conflict situations?
   a. I get angry easily.
   b. I feel nervous and threatened.
   c. I feel like I must have done something wrong.
   d. I stay calm and detached.
   e. Other _____.

3. What economic problems had developed over time in the Jewish community (Neh. 5:1-5)?

4. What was Nehemiah's immediate response to news of economic injustices (v. 6)? How did he channel that immediate response (v. 7)?

5. What charges did Nehemiah bring against the nobles and officials (vv. 7-8)?

6. How did he motivate them to change their business practices (vv. 8-10)?

7. What did Nehemiah demand from the nobles and officials (v. 11)?

8. How did Nehemiah make sure the nobles and officials would do what they promised (vv. 12-13)?

9. What do you most admire about the way Nehemiah handled this conflict situation?

GOING DEEPER

10. What conflicts are you tempted to ignore at home? At work? At church?

11. How should you approach the conflicts differently that you mentioned in question 10 at home? At work? At church?

12. What are the strengths of the example you set in the way you treat people? What are the weaknesses of the example you set in the way you treat people?

CARING TIME

Let's focus our attention on how we deal with conflict within our families. As men, we need to accept responsibility for setting a Christ-like standard in the way we serve and lead those in our household.

1. What conflicts are most likely to occur within your particular family?

2. How do you tend to react emotionally to these conflict situations? How can you step back and gain a more balanced perspective on these conflicts so your emotions don't aggravate them?

3. What kind of example do you need to set in your family to help resolve these conflicts? What is one thing you can change in the coming week to become a better example?

NEXT WEEK

Next week we will see how the Persian king Artaxerxes made Nehemiah governor of the province of Judah. Originally, the emperor's concern had been how quickly Nehemiah could complete his project and return to the palace (2:6). Once he heard about the kind of leadership Nehemiah provided in Judah, the emperor wanted him to remain there. For 12 years, Nehemiah selflessly served the Jews of Judah and Jerusalem. He exemplifies to us all how to accept promotion and success.

SCRIPTURE NOTES

NEHEMIAH 5:1-13

5:1 people and their wives. Stress produced complaints. While working on the walls, families were unable to tend their crops. Complaints from within the group were as hard for Nehemiah to deal with as outside opposition.

5:3 mortgaging our fields. Some workers had mortgaged their fields and vineyards to buy grain. The Jews charged each other exorbitant interest rates.

5:9 walk in the fear of our God and not invite the reproach. Nehemiah became angry, but instead of taking immediate action, he reflected on the problem and cooled down. He was then able to decide on a course of action. He exhorted the people to honor God during the difficult work.

5:10 let us stop charging this interest. As governor, Nehemiah could have acquired real estate and sold it at a profit. Instead, he lent money and grain to the people out of his personal resources. He did not ask the people to sacrifice for the work without setting an example of sacrifice himself.

Personal Notes

CATCHING THE VIEW FROM THE TOP

LAST WEEK

Last week we saw that Nehemiah had more than hostile neighbors with which to contend. Even as he posted guards and prepared the wall builders to double as soldiers, he had to face a major internal conflict between the richest and poorest residents of Jerusalem and Judah. Nehemiah faced the problem head on. He showed great wisdom when he allowed himself time for his anger to cool down so he could gain perspective on the conflict. He then modeled the kind of compassion and concern for the poor that he asked of the rich creditors.

ICEBREAKER

Position and power often go to peoples' heads. This starts when we're young and immature. Supposedly, age and maturity prepare us to handle position and power. Sometimes it does, and sometimes it doesn't.

1. When you were in high school, who was the most popular boy in your class? How did your popularity compare to his?

2. Which of these positions did you have the first time you were in charge of other people? How well did you do as a leader?
   a. A class officer in school
   b. A youth-group leader at church
   c. Captain of a ball team
   d. An officer of a club
   e. A supervisor at work
   f. Other _____

3. Excluding your present one, who is the most obnoxious boss for whom you have worked? What qualities made this person an unpleasant supervisor?

Shortly after Nehemiah arrived in Jerusalem to tackle the security of that city and the social stability of the entire Jewish settlement in Judah, Artaxerxes, the king of Persia, appointed him governor of Judah. Nehemiah's short-term assignment in his native land became an open-ended government position that stretched on for 12 years. We will see in Nehemiah 13 that later he even returned for a second term. How did Nehemiah handle his new position, his new power, and the perks that came with both?

Movin' On Up

[14] Furthermore, from the day King Artaxerxes appointed me to be their governor in the land of Judah—from the twentieth year until his thirty-second year, 12 years—I and my associates never ate from the food allotted to the governor. [15] The governors who preceded me had heavily burdened the people, taking food and wine from them, as well as a pound of silver. Their subordinates also oppressed the people, but I didn't do this, because of the fear of God. [16] Instead, I devoted myself to the construction of the wall, and all my subordinates were gathered there for the work. We didn't buy any land.

[17] There were 150 Jews and officials, as well as guests from the surrounding nations at my table. [18] Each day, one ox, six choice sheep, and some fowl were prepared for me. An abundance of all kinds of wine was [provided] every 10 days. But I didn't demand the food allotted to the governor, because the burden on the people was so heavy.

[19] Remember me favorably, my God, for all that I have done for this people.

Nehemiah 5:14-19

PRINCIPLES TO LIVE BY

Nehemiah's experience and example as governor of Judah speaks clearly to every one of us as we live and work in our various communities. If we do our jobs well, we'll normally experience advancement, which brings increased responsibilities. It is part of our social and economic system, and we certainly wouldn't want it any other way. But how can we accept promotion with a proper Christian perspective?

PRINCIPLE 1

WE SHOULD CONSIDER ACCEPTING A PROMOTION AS A POTENTIAL BLESSING FROM GOD, AND CONSIDER WHETHER IT MIGHT BE HIS WAY AND HIS TIMING FOR EXPANDING OUR INFLUENCE.

Some Christians are afraid of advancement, particularly to positions that involve authority and increased responsibility. Perhaps they fear failure. Perhaps they feel that advancement is somehow wrong and inappropriate for God's children. It just seems too worldly. These, however, are not valid reasons for rejecting a promotion.

We, of course, should count the costs of a promotion. For example, if increased time demands have the potential to harm our families or our spiritual priorities, we should think very carefully before accepting this kind of advancement. We may need to refuse the offer. Ultimately, however, we need to consider what God can do through us if we accept the promotion. Nehemiah evidently felt God was blessing him with the appointment to the post of governor in Judah. He envisioned a number of positive results for his homeland.

PRINCIPLE 2

WE SHOULD CONSIDER ACCEPTING A PROMOTION BECAUSE IT MAY GIVE US AN OPPORTUNITY FOR PERSONAL GROWTH IN CHARACTER AND SKILLS.

Increased leadership responsibility stretches us in a variety of ways. It can increase our faith and teach us to pray more effectively. It will teach us new skills in relating to people and in handling difficult situations. In actuality, increased responsibilities that accompany a promotion will inevitably bring periods of emotional stress, but for most of us, we need a certain amount of anxiety to cause us to grow spiritually and psychologically. We see this in Nehemiah's experience. He obviously matured as a leader because of the challenges he faced—from the time he received the report regarding the plight of his people until he helped them rebuild the wall.

WE SHOULD CONSIDER ACCEPTING A PROMOTION BECAUSE IT MAY BE GOD'S WAY TO IMPROVE OUR FINANCIAL SITUATION.

When we earn enough to live comfortably, it frees us from worry and concern. Our security in life increases. This allows us to be more productive. Rather than dissipating our energy through worry, we can focus our energy on honoring and glorifying God. An increased income also enables us to give more to meet the needs of others and to advance the work of God.

Nehemiah's promotion to the post of governor apparently followed other promotions that had made him wealthy. True to His godly character, He actually deferred the financial perks of his new position as a primary way of helping his fellow Jews (vv. 15, 18).

PRINCIPLE 4

WE SHOULD CONSIDER ACCEPTING A PROMOTION SINCE IT MAY PROVIDE US WITH AN OPPORTUNITY TO CREATE WORKING CONDITIONS THAT WILL BENEFIT AND HELP OTHERS.

Nehemiah was sensitive to the needs of the Jewish people he governed. He knew they had been struggling for years against the enemies around them. He knew morale among the people was alarmingly low. They barely had enough food to survive. They were hanging on by their fingernails economically, and now he was demanding their time to rebuild the walls.

Nehemiah's conscience would not let him lay any extra burdens on the Jewish people. The first part of Nehemiah 5 details how he used his authority as governor to alleviate the injustices caused by the oppressive lending policies of the upper class in Jerusalem. The second part of the chapter tells how Nehemiah refused to levy taxes on the citizenry to support his administration. He genuinely wanted to improve peoples' positions in life.

LESSON 9

PRINCIPLE 5

WHEN WE ACCEPT A PROMOTION, WE MUST REALIZE THAT WE WILL FACE NEW TEMPTATIONS, AND BRACE OURSELVES SO WE DON'T FALL FLAT.

The governors before Nehemiah all had used their position to advance their personal wealth and comfort (v. 15). The people expected Nehemiah to gouge them and use his office for his own advantage. A lesser man would have yielded to this temptation.

We need to be on guard about the dangers inherent in new powers, freedoms, and privileges that may accompany our promotions. We need humility and a sense of godly purpose to avoid the lures of pride and greed.

PRINCIPLE 6

WHEN PROMOTED, WE MUST NEVER ABUSE OUR PRIVILEGES TO BUILD OUR OWN EMPIRES.

Once promoted to the governor's seat, previous governors in Jerusalem had set out to "promote" themselves. Nehemiah refused to fall prey to selfish ambition. He didn't send his staff out to raise revenue and feather their nests. Initially he involved his staff in building the walls. Later he engaged them in renewing the commitment of the Jews to the Law of God (chapters 8–12).

Most everyone promoted to a position in top management in our culture faces temptations to abuse that power. We need to be committed to the values of God's Word so we don't misuse our expense accounts, exploit subordinates, and use company time to build our own personal empire.

PRINCIPLE 7

WHEN PROMOTED, WE MIGHT BE WISE TO GIVE UP CERTAIN RIGHTS TO AVOID ANY "APPEARANCE OF EVIL," OR SIMPLY TO BE A GOOD EXAMPLE.

Nehemiah gave up his right to use the governor's food allowance (v. 18) and to collect at least some of the taxes other governors had imposed (v. 15). He gave up these rights because the people were facing hard economic times. He was asking them to sacrifice personally in order to rebuild the walls, so he chose to sacrifice some of his own rights in response to them.

The Apostle Paul wrote the Corinthians, "If we have sown spiritual things for you, is it too much if we reap material things from you? If others share this authority over you, don't we even more? However, we have not used this authority; instead we endure everything so that we will not hinder the gospel of Christ" (1 Cor. 9:11-12). There are times when we too should be prepared to give up our rights to avoid being misinterpreted and to lead well.

PRINCIPLE 8

WE SHOULD ONLY ACCEPT A PROMOTION WITH PROPER MOTIVES.

Three factors motivated Nehemiah as he carried out the work of governor. He feared God (v. 15), he was sensitive to peoples' needs (v. 18), and he desired God's special blessing in his life (v. 19). If we approach advancement and promotion with these same basic motivations, we too will have the keys to maintaining our spiritual and psychological equilibrium.

QUESTIONS FOR INTERACTION

1. What does it take in your line of work to earn promotions?

2. Select the statement that best expresses your expectation of promotion:
   a. If I work hard, I'll be promoted.
   b. If I play the company political games, I may be promoted.
   c. I've probably advanced as far as I'm going.
   d. I have no ambitions to be promoted.
   e. Other _____.

3. While Nehemiah was governor of Judah, how did he show his concern for his people (vv. 14, 16, 18b)?

4. How had the previous governors mistreated the Jews (v. 15)?

5. How do we know that Nehemiah went to great personal expense to keep from burdening the Jews financially (vv. 17-18)?

6. What motivated Nehemiah to behave as he did (vv. 15b, 18b)?

7. Why do you think Nehemiah prayed as he did in verse 19?

8. How does your work give you the opportunity to serve other people?

9. If your employer promoted you, how could you serve others better?

GOING DEEPER

10. How would a promotion at work (or in your church) stretch you as a person?

11. What new temptations would you face if you received a promotion?

12. If you were promoted at work (or church), what privileges would you think twice about using in order to set a good example?

 ## CARING TIME

Advancement in the workplace doesn't look the same for everyone. Management often looks for a corner office and a golden parachute. Labor naturally works toward seniority and higher skill classifications. Predictably, professionals try to land bigger contracts and gain the respect of their colleagues. Every man in this room would define advancement differently. We probably all have different thoughts about what we want from our careers.

1. How do you feel about your prospects for advancement in your present job? Are you happy with these prospects?

2. In your employment, do you face the future with positive expectations or with serious concerns, and why?

3. Pray for the man to your right, asking God either to bless his expectations or to give him wisdom in dealing with his concerns.

NEXT WEEK

Next week we'll look at a final burst of opposition that erupted as the walls of Jerusalem neared completion. Only the doors remained to be hung in the gates. Nehemiah's opponents seized the last window of opportunity to remove him from the picture or to ruin his reputation and compromise his influence. Their plans were slick, but we'll see how Nehemiah kept his eyes on the Lord and on the work He had given him to do.

NEHEMIAH 5:14-19

5:14 12 years. During his 12 years as governor, Nehemiah collected no taxes from the people as he could have done.

5:16 devoted myself. He could have lent money with real estate as security, and then foreclosed when the people could not repay their debts. However, Nehemiah remembered that his purpose was to help the people, not to exploit them. He was careful not to abuse his position as governor.

5:17 guests from the surrounding nations at my table. A ruler was expected to entertain lavishly. Nehemiah served visiting officials from his own food and wine.

5:18 the food allotted to the governor. Aware of the deprivations of his people, Nehemiah did not use the provisions to which he, as governor, would have been entitled.

PERSONAL NOTES

LESSON 9

BLUNTING THE CHISEL OF CRITICISM

LAST WEEK

Last week we observed that King Artaxerxes quickly promoted Nehemiah to the position of governor of Judah based on his excellent leadership during the wall-building project. He approached his new work with a servant spirit. He cared more about the needs of the people than about advancing his own prestige and wealth. If we achieve a promotion, we too should evaluate our opportunities in terms of God's priorities for our lives and in terms of what God can do through us in the new position.

ICEBREAKER

When we were kids on the playground and someone called us names, we'd chant, "Sticks and stones may break my bones, but words will never hurt me!" In reality, we sometimes felt like chanting, "Sticks and stones may break my bones, but your words are killing me!" You may still remember the kids who specialized in cruel words.

1. What's the meanest name anyone called you when you were growing up? How did you respond to that?

2. Tell about a time you "tattled" on someone to get him or her into trouble. Why did you do it? What happened?

3. When do you first remember seeing adults (beside your parents) extremely mad at one another? How did you feel about their anger?

BIBLICAL FOUNDATION

In Nehemiah 6, Sanballat, Tobiah, and Geshem made one final effort to keep Nehemiah from hanging the doors in the gates and completing the walls of Jerusalem. It was their most subtle and insidious attack, and Nehemiah was their sole object. If they could get to him personally, they might have a chance once again to demoralize the people. This chapter describes three subtle attacks on Nehemiah. Each was different, but each was designed to destroy him. If they could not take his life, they would settle for undermining his effectiveness as a leader in Israel.

Last Gasp Intimidation

[1] When Sanballat, Tobiah, Geshem the Arab, and the rest of our enemies heard that I had rebuilt the wall and that no gap was left in it—though at that time I had not installed the doors in the gates— [2] Sanballat and Geshem sent me a message: "Come, let's meet together in the villages of the Ono Valley." But they were planning to harm me.

[3] So I sent messengers to them, saying, "I am doing a great work and cannot come down. Why should the work cease while I leave it and go down to you?" [4] Four times they sent me the same proposal, and I gave them the same reply.

[5] Sanballat sent me this same message a fifth time by his aide, who had an open letter in his hand. [6] In it was written:

It is reported among the nations—and Geshem agrees—that you and the Jews plan to rebel. This is the reason you are building the wall. According to these reports, you are to become their king [7] and have even set up the prophets in Jerusalem to proclaim on your behalf: "There is a king in Judah." These rumors will be heard by the king. So come, let's confer together.

[8] Then I replied to him, "There is nothing to these rumors you are spreading; you are inventing them in your own mind." [9] For they were all trying to intimidate us, saying, "They will become discouraged in the work, and it will never be finished."

But now, [my God,] strengthen me.

[10] I went to the house of Shemaiah son of Delaiah, son of Mehetabel, who was restricted [to his house]. He said:

> Let us meet at the house of God
> inside the temple.
> Let us shut the temple doors
> because they are coming to kill you.
> They are coming to kill you tonight!

[11] But I said, "Should a man like me run away? How can I enter the temple and live? I will not go." [12] I realized that God had not sent him, because of the prophecy he spoke against me. Tobiah and Sanballat had hired him. [13] He was hired, so that I would be intimidated, do as he suggested, sin, and get a bad reputation, in order that they could discredit me.

[14] My God, remember Tobiah and Sanballat for what they have done, and also Noadiah the prophetess and the other prophets who wanted to intimidate me.

Nehemiah 6:1-14

PRINCIPLES TO LIVE BY

Most of us cannot identify with Nehemiah's frustrating encounters with Sanballat, Tobiah, and Geshem. There are few of us living in our culture today who face threats on our lives. In fact, very few of us have enemies who deliberately and maliciously attempt to destroy our reputation and credibility, although there are some instances when this happens.

Once again, Nehemiah's responses yield some powerful principles to live by. *How* he faced these problems exemplifies for us how we can respond to all levels of human conflict, whether it involves a deceptive and malicious attack on one end of the conflict continuum, or naïve and sincere criticism on the opposite end.

PRINCIPLE 1

WHEN WE ARE CRITICIZED, WE MUST NOT COUNTERATTACK BY CHALLENGING THE OTHER PERSON'S MOTIVES.

First, Sanballat and Geshem tried to get Nehemiah away from the security of Jerusalem on the pretext of holding a peace conference in the Ono Valley some 25 miles northwest of the city (v. 2). Nehemiah never challenged the intentions of his enemies. Four times, he simply but firmly refused because he could not leave the work at such a critical phase (vv. 3-4).

Perhaps the one criticizing us has wrong motives. In most instances though, we can't prove it. It's best to busy ourselves with the work God has given us and politely refuse to be dragged into risky encounters with our critics. Sometimes, what appears to be an inappropriate motive on the part of a critic may actually be sincere. We need to allow for that possibility.

PRINCIPLE 2

WE MUST BE PATIENT AND WAIT FOR OUR CRITIC'S MOTIVES TO BE REVEALED, AVOIDING A DEFENSIVE POSTURE.

After four failed attempts to lure Nehemiah away from Jerusalem to a bogus peace conference, Sanballat and Geshem changed their strategy. They sent a messenger to read in public charges of treason against Nehemiah. Now they demanded that he meet them to answer their charges (vv. 5-7). Finally, the enemies had revealed how they really felt about Nehemiah.

Conflicts inevitably arise when people live and work together. When they do, we need to wait patiently for the motives of critics to become clear. Most Christians are not out to hurt or harm other Christians. They think they are helping by pointing out a problem in the church. If people are critical because they're sincerely naïve, they'll normally have a change of heart if we continue to be open, sincere, and non-defensive. As we are patient, any truly malicious and false motives will eventually come to the surface and we can respond appropriately both to our critics and to our supporters.

PRINCIPLE 3

WHEN CRITICIZED BY NON-CHRISTIANS, WE SHOULD RESPOND AS JESUS TAUGHT—WITH GENTLENESS AND RESPECT. PERHAPS OUR RESPONSE WILL SHED THE LIGHT OF GOD'S TRUTH AND LOVE IN THEIR LIVES.

The Apostle Peter applied the teaching of Jesus to first-century Christians scattered throughout various sections of the Eastern Mediterranean world. We too should heed his teaching.

> Conduct yourselves honorably among the Gentiles, *so that in a case where they speak against you* as those who do evil, they may, by observing your good works, glorify God in a day of visitation … for it is God's will that you, by doing good, silence the ignorance of foolish people (1 Pet. 2:12,15).

> But set apart the Messiah as Lord in your hearts, and always be ready to give a defense to anyone who asks you for a reason for the hope that is in you. However, do this with gentleness and respect, keeping your conscience clear, *so that when you are accused*, those who denounce your Christian life will be put to shame (1 Pet. 3:15-16).

PRINCIPLE 4

WHEN CRITICIZED UNJUSTLY, WE MUST BE BOLD AND HONEST IN OUR RESPONSES TO RUMORS, YET WE SHOULD NEVER TAKE REVENGE.

Nehemiah's enemies tried to harm him by starting a rumor they hoped would force him to meet with them. His response outlines a very biblical way for us to handle this kind of public pressure. First, he denied the false accusations with a straightforward but non-defensive response (v. 8). Second, he interpreted what had happened in the hearing of those closest to him so they could know the truth (v. 9a). Third, he prayed for personal strength to endure the anxiety and stress caused by these false rumors (v. 9b).

LESSON 10

WHEN FALSELY ACCUSED, WE MUST NOT ALLOW FEAR TO CLOUD
OUR PERCEPTIONS SO THAT WE ACT IMPULSIVELY AND DO
SOMETHING FOOLISH.

Nehemiah's enemies wanted to frighten him, particularly when they
told him King Artaxerxes would hear these reports (v. 7). Later, they used
a false prophecy concerning threats on his life to prompt him to behave in
a cowardly manner (v. 10). Through it all, Nehemiah did not allow his fear
to cause him to act irrationally.

When criticized, we can spend all our time and energy protecting
our images, all the while being sidetracked from our primary work and
responsibility. Instead, we should imitate Jesus, "who for the joy that lay
before him endured a cross and despised the shame .... For consider Him
who endured such hostility from sinners against Himself, so that you
won't grow weary and lose heart" (Heb. 12:2-3).

PRINCIPLE 6

WHEN WE FOLLOW GOD'S PRINCIPLES FOR HANDLING FALSE
ACCUSATIONS, HE WILL UPHOLD US THROUGH OUR TRIALS AND,
ULTIMATELY, DEFEND US.

Nehemiah turned to God and delivered his enemies and their wicked
schemes over to Him (v. 14). He named his chief tormentors—Sanballat,
Tobiah, and a prophetess named Noadiah whose part in all this we don't
know. He included all the other enemies with the traitorous prophets who
tried to convince him God wanted him to give up.

Can you imagine how hard it had been for Nehemiah to maintain
his confidence in God's call to build those walls in the face of such an
organized campaign of intimidation? He didn't do it through human
wisdom and strength. He relied on God's prudence, power, and
protection.

QUESTIONS FOR INTERACTION

1. How do you think you would fare if you had to deal with all the
   pressure Nehemiah experienced in chapter 6:1-14?

2. Which of these kinds of pressure troubles you most, and why?
    a. Pressure from people or circumstances on the outside of my circle
    b. Pressure from people or circumstances on the inside of my circle
    c. Pressure I generate myself through worry and anxiety
    d. Other _____

3. Why were the enemies of Nehemiah intent on attacking him fiercely before the doors were hung in the gates (v. 1)?

4. What did Sanballat and Geshem hope to accomplish by inviting Nehemiah to a conference in the Ono Valley (vv. 2-4)?

5. What did Sanballat and Geshem hope to accomplish by publicly accusing Nehemiah of rebelling against the Persian emperor (vv. 5-9)?

6. How would Nehemiah have violated the Law if he had fled into the temple (v. 10; Num. 3:10; 18:7)?

7. What would have happened to Nehemiah's reputation if he had taken refuge in the temple (v. 13)

8. Why do you think Nehemiah included his prayers in the record he made of his activities in Jerusalem (1:5-11; 2:4; 4:4-5; 5:19; 6:9,14)?

9. What is the most important lesson you learned from Nehemiah in this chapter about responding to criticism?

GOING DEEPER

10. Why is it important to be patient when falsely accused and not respond immediately to your critics?

11. How should we respond when criticized by unbelievers?

12. Why must we be careful about responding out of fear to those who criticize us?

 CARING TIME

Most of us don't like criticism for the way we do things, and especially false accusations. However, at times we all must deal with misunderstanding and opposition. When we do, we need to avoid self-pity. We must refuse to withdraw from people and sulk. We need to control our anger and not lash out. We need to help one another grow into the kind of men who respond maturely as Nehemiah did.

1. What positive lessons have you learned through dealing with criticism in your life?

2. What present situations concern you as possible sources of misunderstanding or criticism?

3. Pray for the man to your left, asking God to protect him and grant him wisdom to deal with misunderstanding or criticism in the setting he identified in question 2.

NEXT WEEK

Next week we will turn from the completed walls of Jerusalem to examine the spiritual renewal of the people living in and around Jerusalem. Nehemiah partnered with the scribe Ezra to reacquaint the Jews with the Law of God. The people were thrilled because the walls were rebuilt, and they gathered for a national assembly. They called on Ezra and his disciples to read and explain the covenant God had made with Israel at Mount Sinai. The Jews responded with sorrowful repentance that Nehemiah channeled into joyful obedience.

SCRIPTURE NOTES

NEHEMIAH 6:1-14

6:1 gates. Gates were small fortresses guarding the entry points through a defensive wall. One set of heavy wooden doors entered the "gate" from the outside, and another set exited the "gate" into the city. Interior walls interrupted straight lines of sight and movement through the "gate." Guards were stationed inside the gate and on its roof. Those atop the gate could fire arrows down into it.

6:2 let's meet together. When Nehemiah's enemies heard that the wall was nearly completed, they set a trap for him as another attempt to stop the work. (An example of Proverbs 26:24-25.) They invited him to meet them 25 miles northwest of Jerusalem, a day's journey.

6:3 Why should the work cease? Nehemiah wisely refused to leave the work unsupervised for he did not want to be distracted, but he did not accuse his enemies outright of planning harm.

6:4 Four times they sent me. The adversaries were persistent and unyielding, and through this they revealed their true motives. If they sincerely wanted peace, they could have come to Jerusalem to meet him.

6:5 an open letter in his hand. Failing to entice Nehemiah into their trap, the enemies resorted to accusations that Nehemiah planned to overthrow King Artaxerxes. Since the letter was unsealed, it was obviously meant to be read, and the rumor spread.

6:8 you are inventing them. Nehemiah's response is bold and direct. He explained the lie to the Jewish workers. He also prayed for strength.

6:10 Shemaiah … was restricted to his house. To lure Nehemiah into the temple, his enemies hired this priest who claimed to be a prophet. He tried to frighten Nehemiah into hiding from assassins in the holy place, which was forbidden by the Law (Num. 3:10; 18:7).

6:11 I will not go. He realized that God would not tell him to flee when the wall was nearly completed.

6:12 God had not sent him. Nehemiah knew that a true prophet would not advise someone to desecrate the sanctuary by disobeying the Law.

6:13 discredit me. Nehemiah recognized the danger to the project if he were to run and hide out of fear. Morale among the people would have plummeted.

REMODELING THE INTERIOR ... USING BIBLICAL BLUEPRINTS

LAST WEEK

Last week we saw how Nehemiah focused on hanging the doors in the gates to finish the wall project in the face of a flurry of initiatives by his enemies to destroy or discredit him. He ignored their tricks, denied their false accusations, and saw through the deceit of people he thought were his friends. He handled all these criticisms and false accusations patiently, honestly, and in reliance on the Lord. We saw that we too must not let criticism and false accusations defeat or frustrate us. We must respond as Jesus taught and trust the Father to vindicate us.

ICEBREAKER

Once upon a time, most people in our culture grew up with some exposure to Bible stories and had a rudimentary sense of major Christian concepts. Those days are gone. Many people reach adulthood with little or no knowledge of the Bible. Even many regular churchgoers have decided the Bible is too big, too old, and too intimidating for them to understand.

1. Which of these statements best describes how you were first acquainted with the Bible?
   a. I grew up in Sunday School, hearing the Bible stories and learning memory verses.
   b. I got interested in the Bible during high school or college.
   c. I started reading the Bible after I became a Christian as an adult.
   d. I still know very little about the Bible.
   e. Other _____.

2. Which of these statements accurately reports something the Bible says?
   a. Moses took two of every kind of animal into the ark.
   b. Samson was a Nazirite; Jesus was a Nazarene.
   c. Angels sang God's praises to the shepherds the night Jesus was born.
   d. An epistle was the wife of an apostle.

3. Tell of an incident when your lack of Bible knowledge kept you from helping someone or from accomplishing something.

BIBLICAL FOUNDATION

Very few key leaders ever succeed in isolation. Moses had Aaron and later Joshua; Joshua had Caleb; Elijah had Elisha; Peter had John; Paul had Barnabas and later Silas. Though it may appear that Nehemiah completed his task alone, that was not the case. He would have been the first to pay a great tribute to Ezra, the man who arrived in Jerusalem 13 years before Nehemiah came on the scene. This old scribe had laid the foundation for Nehemiah's success, not in terms of bricks and stones, but in terms of the Law of God. The people paid tribute to Ezra when they held a solemn assembly to thank God for the completion of the walls.

Encountering the Law of God

Chapter 8

When the seventh month came and the Israelites had settled in their towns, [1] all the people gathered together at the square in front of the Water Gate. They asked Ezra the scribe to bring the book of the law of Moses that the LORD had given Israel. [2] On the first day of the seventh month, Ezra the priest brought the law before the assembly of men, women, and all who could listen with understanding. [3] While he was facing the square in front of the Water Gate, he read out of it from daybreak until noon before the men, the women, and those who could understand. All the people listened attentively to the book of the law. [4] Ezra the scribe stood on a high wooden platform made for this purpose. …. [5] Ezra opened the book in full view of all the people, since he was elevated above everyone. As he opened it, all the people stood up. [6] Ezra blessed the LORD, the great God, and with their hands uplifted all the people said, " Amen, Amen!" Then they bowed down and worshiped the LORD with their faces to the ground.

[7] [The Levites] explained the law to the people as they stood in their places. [8] They read the book of the law of God, translating and giving the meaning so that the people could understand what was read. [9] Nehemiah the governor, Ezra the priest and scribe, and the Levites who were instructing the people said to all of them, "This day is holy to the LORD your God. Do not mourn or weep." For all the people were weeping as they heard the words of the law. [10] Then he said to them, "Go and eat what is rich, drink what is sweet, and send portions to those who

have nothing prepared, since today is holy to our Lord. Do not grieve, because your strength [comes from] rejoicing in the LORD." [11] And the Levites quieted all the people, saying, "Be still, since today is holy. Do not grieve." [12] Then all the people began to eat and drink, send portions, and have a great celebration, because they had understood the words that were explained to them.

[13] On the second day, the family leaders of all the people, along with the priests and Levites, assembled before Ezra the scribe to study the words of the law. [14] They found written in the law how the LORD had commanded through Moses that the Israelites should dwell in booths during the festival of the seventh month. ... [17] The whole community that had returned from exile made booths and lived in them. They had not celebrated like this from the days of Joshua son of Nun until that day. And there was tremendous joy. [18] Ezra read out of the book of the law of God every day, from the first day to the last. The Israelites celebrated the feast for seven days, and on the eighth day there was an assembly, according to the ordinance.

Chapter 9

[1] On the twenty-fourth day of this month the Israelites assembled; they were fasting, [wearing] sackcloth, [and had put] dust on their heads. [2] Those of Israelite descent separated themselves from all foreigners, and they stood and confessed their sins and the guilt of their fathers. [3] While they stood in their places, they read from the book of the law of the LORD their God for a fourth of the day and [spent] another fourth of the day in confession and worship of the LORD their God.

Nehemiah 8:1-4a, 5-6, 7b-14; 8:17–9:3

PRINCIPLES TO LIVE BY

As we apply our study of this encounter of the Jews with the Law of God, let's focus on divine principles that relate to the Word of God in our lives. After all, the Scriptures were foundational in bringing renewal to Israel. Without this foundation that Ezra laid, Nehemiah could not possibly have succeeded in rebuilding the walls in 52 days (6:15). Furthermore, he would have had a terrible time dealing with social injustice in Israel (5:1-13).

THE BIBLE CONTAINS GOD'S COMPLETE WRITTEN REVELATION, SO WE SHOULD BE EAGER TO READ IT, UNDERSTAND IT, AND APPLY IT TO OUR LIVES.

During the 13 years before Nehemiah came to Jerusalem (compare Ezra 7:8 and Neh. 2:1), a scribe named Ezra had taught the Law of God to the Jews in Judah (Ezra 7:10). When he first arrived, the spiritual apathy of the people and the ungodliness of their lives appalled him (Ezra 9:3, 6). Gradually, through the quality of his example and the intensity of his teaching, Ezra had made an impact. When Nehemiah challenged them to rebuild the wall, they were prepared to accept the challenge.

Once the walls were completed, the people celebrated by calling on Ezra to read them "the book of the law of Moses" (8:1). As Ezra read, the Levites who assisted him translated the Hebrew for those who no longer spoke the native tongue and explained the difficulties of the biblical text (8:7-8).

We are indeed fortunate. Not only do we have access to the Old Testament, but we also have at our disposal God's complete written revelation in our language. Furthermore, in recent years modern translations have multiplied, causing the Scriptures to come alive with meaning. We are no longer locked in, needing someone to "translate" and interpret languages we don't understand.

PRINCIPLE 2

WE MUST DETERMINE IN OUR HEARTS TO DEVOTE OURSELVES TO A SERIOUS STUDY OF THE BIBLE IF WE WANT A DYNAMIC RELATIONSHIP WITH GOD.

Ezra was deeply committed to understanding and obeying God's will. More than that, he was committed to teaching others the will of God. "Ezra had determined in his heart to study the law of the LORD, obey it, and teach its statutes and ordinances in Israel" (Ezra 7:10). Ezra had a dynamic relationship with the God he loved.

Many of us do not study the Bible regularly on our own. First, we don't know how. Second, we're terribly busy. As a result, we simply neglect this unique opportunity and responsibility. We try it now and then, get discouraged, and give up. This leaves us biblically illiterate and seriously malnourished spiritually.

We need a method for getting into the Word of God. Here are some preliminary steps to take:

LESSON 11

1. Determine that you *are* going to study the Bible regularly.
2. Decide on a study time that fits your personal schedule.
3. Choose the place that's best for you.
4. Select a good literal, but modern Bible translation such as the New International Version˚, Holman Christian Standard Bible˚, New King James Version, New Living Translation, or English Standard Version™.
5. Use a study guide that is (1) simple and practical, (2) flexible to fit your schedule, and (3) helpful as you read, interpret, and apply the passage.
6. Purchase a notebook in which you can record the key revelations and results of your study.
7. Select and purchase a quality hymnal (or a worship song book or CD) you can use for meditation, worship, and praise.

PRINCIPLE 3

TO GET THE MOST FROM OUR STUDY OF THE BIBLE, WE MUST LEARN EFFECTIVE METHODS AND STRATEGIES.

When the Jews heard Ezra read the Law, they began to weep in remorse because they realized they were not living in obedience to it (8:9). Nehemiah, Ezra, and the other leaders quickly pointed out that the Law instructed God's people to celebrate the Feast of Tabernacles at that time in the seventh month. The appropriate emotion for that festival was joy (8:10). The Jews had not been keeping the annual festivals. They did not know the Law or how to study it. Ezra's scribes and Levites would need to teach them in the years that followed.

Here are eight simple steps we can follow for effective Bible study:

1. *Pray.* Praise God and ask the Holy Spirit to illumine your mind.
2. *Survey.* Read the passage quickly to get the "big picture" prior to studying its parts.
3. *Read.* Read the passage carefully.
4. *Observe.* Look for the details of the text that are important to understand.
5. *Interpret.* Ask and attempt to answer the question, "What does this mean?" concerning the details you observed in Step 4.
6. *Apply.* Consider the implications of this passage for your life. Choose responses you sense God wants you to make in obedience to His Word.
7. *Pray.* Talk with God about the meaning and the application of His Word. Tell Him you want to obey. Ask for His help. Pray for others in terms of the truth of the passage you studied.
8. *Share.* Look for a natural opportunity to encourage someone with what you learned.

QUESTIONS FOR INTERACTION

1. What are your biggest obstacles to studying the Bible?

2. What has been the greatest help you've received in studying the Bible? How did this benefit you?

3. To whom did Ezra read the Law (Neh. 7:66-67; 8:2)?

4. Where did the people gather to hear the Law read (8:1; see the map in Lesson 4)?

5. What role did the Levites play in the reading of the Law (8:7-8)?

6. Why did Nehemiah, Ezra, and the other leaders redirect the mourning of the people into joyous celebration (8:9-12)?

7. The family leaders discovered the teaching about the Feast of Tabernacles in their own study of the Law (8:13-18). What difference do you think that made in the way they celebrated it?

8. What role did the Word of God play in the Jewish revival at the end of the seventh month (9:1-3)?

9. Which do you think gave the Jews greater security: rebuilding their walls or renewing their relationship with God, and why?

GOING DEEPER

10. Which translations of the Bible do you find most helpful, and why?

11. What adjustments would you need to make to your schedule to do regular Bible study?

12. When you look at the Bible study method in Principle 3, with which step do you need the most help, and why?

 CARING TIME

Each man in our group probably has reacted differently to this lesson about Bible study. We have different levels of Bible knowledge. We have different levels of interest in activities that involve reading books. Some of us are left-brain types that approach the Bible as information to master and organize. Some of us are right-brain guys who approach the Bible as literature to grasp imaginatively. However, all of us want to meet God in His Word and respond to Him in worship and obedience.

1. What changes are you hoping to make in your Bible reading and study because of this lesson?

2. If you run into a question during your study, who in our group might you call? Which church leader might you call?

3. Pray within the group that each man would grow in his Bible study skills and in his commitment to personal Bible study.

NEXT WEEK

Next week we will look at the last chapter of the Book of Nehemiah. Nehemiah had returned to Persia after 12 years as governor of Judah. Some time later he returned to see how things fared in the province he had left in such excellent physical and spiritual condition. To his dismay, conditions had decayed dramatically. We'll watch as this strong leader confronts and rebukes spiritual and moral laxness within God's people.

SCRIPTURE NOTES

NEHEMIAH 8:1-3, 10-17; 9:3

8:1 all the people gathered together. The people from the cities and countryside of Judah gathered to hear Ezra read and teach the Law in the five books of Moses (Deut. 31:11-12). **Water Gate.** They met in an open square between the southeast part of the temple and the eastern wall.

8:2 first day of the seventh month, Ezra the priest. Taking place in the September-October period, this was the Feast of Trumpets, where work stopped and a sacred assembly took place.

8:3 read out of it from daybreak until noon. Adults and children who were old enough to understand (vv. 2-3) stood and listened attentively all morning.

8:10 Go and eat what is rich. When they heard the Law read and explained, the people wept and repented of their sins. While the Israelite's response undoubtedly pleased Nehemiah, he reminded them that it was a time to celebrate with feasting.

8:17 the days of Joshua ... until that day. The joy and involvement of this celebration was unmatched since Joshua's day, because the people themselves had helped reconstruct the walls.

9:1 fasting ... sackcloth ... dust. These actions symbolized remorse and grief over sin. Sackcloth was a dark, coarse cloth made from goat's hair (Pss. 30:11; 35:13). Dust referred to ashes (1 Sam. 4:12).

PERSONAL NOTES

NAILING DOWN OBEDIENCE

LAST WEEK

Last week we saw that Nehemiah's success in building the walls of Jerusalem depended on the Bible teaching ministry of Ezra during the 14 years prior to Nehemiah's arrival. Once the walls were completed, the populace of Jerusalem and surrounding areas gathered in a public square to hear Ezra read the Law of God. In response to the Law, the people repented of their sins, celebrated the joyous Feast of Tabernacles, and renewed their covenant with the Lord. At this point, both the physical and spiritual "walls" of Jerusalem stood restored and strong.

ICEBREAKER

The ancient Greeks told a story called "The Myth of Sisyphus." Sisyphus was doomed to spend eternity in Hades trying to roll a boulder up a steep hillside. Every time he strained and groaned to the top of the hill, he lost control of his boulder, and it rolled clear to the bottom of the slope. Fate forced him to start again, only to fail once more at the last instant.

Sisyphus reminds us how horrible and frustrating it is to near the end of an unpleasant job, only to have it unravel so that we have to do it all over again. This kind of aggravation can test our patience, no matter who we are.

1. Which of these repetitive activities do you like least, and why?
   a. Television reruns
   b. Washing the car
   c. Exercising
   d. Paying bills
   e. Waiting for your favorite team to win the championship "next year"
   f. Other _____

2. Share a time when you lost or incorrectly completed a school assignment and had to do it over again.

3. What repetitive aspect of your job do you wish you could avoid, and why?

It would be nice if Nehemiah's story concluded with a happy ending. Unfortunately, the people of Jerusalem and Judah quickly turned back to their careless, sinful ways after Nehemiah's 12-year term as governor of Judah. The Jews had dedicated the walls of Jerusalem with great pageantry (12:27-43). They had committed themselves to support the temple worship with tithes and offerings (10:32-39). They had renewed their covenant with the Lord, promising to keep the Sabbath and refusing to intermarry with pagan neighbors (10:30-31). The leaders of the people had signed a formal document promising all these things (9:38–10:27).

However, when Nehemiah returned to Jerusalem from Susa after an absence of no more than a year or two, he found a situation that compelled him to beat men and pull hair (13:25). He quickly set about to correct some of the Israelites most grievous sins.

Let's Do It All Again!

⁴ Now before this, Eliashib the priest had been put in charge of the storerooms of the house of our God. He was a relative of Tobiah ⁵ and had prepared a large room for him where they had previously stored the grain offerings, the frankincense, the articles, and the tenths of grain, new wine, and oil prescribed for the Levites, singers, and gatekeepers, along with the contributions for the priests.

⁶ While all this was happening, I was not in Jerusalem, because I had returned to King Artaxerxes of Babylon in the thirty-second year of his [reign]. It was only later that I asked the king for a leave of absence ⁷ so I could return to Jerusalem. Then I discovered the evil that Eliashib had done on behalf of Tobiah by providing him a room in the courts of God's house. ⁸ I was greatly displeased and threw all of Tobiah's household possessions out of the room. ⁹ I ordered that the rooms be purified, and I had the articles of the house of God restored there, along with the grain offering and frankincense. ¹⁰ I also found out that because the portions for the Levites had not been given, each of the Levites and the singers performing the service had gone back to his own field. ¹¹ Therefore, I rebuked the officials, saying, "Why has the house of God been neglected?" I gathered the Levites and singers together and stationed them at their posts. ¹² Then all Judah brought a tenth of the grain, new wine, and oil into the storehouses. ¹³ I appointed as treasurers over the storehouses Shelemiah the priest, Zadok the scribe, and Pedaiah of the Levites, with Hanan son of Zaccur, son of Mattaniah to assist them, because they were considered trustworthy. They were responsible for the distribution to their colleagues.

¹⁴ Remember me for this, my God, and don't erase the good deeds I have done for the house of my God and for its services.

¹⁵ At that time I saw people in Judah treading wine presses on the Sabbath. They were also bringing in stores of grain and loading [them] on donkeys, along with wine, grapes, and figs. All kinds of goods were being brought to Jerusalem on the Sabbath day. So I warned [them] against selling food on that day. ¹⁶ The Tyrians living there were importing fish and all kinds of merchandise and selling them on the Sabbath to the people of Judah in Jerusalem.

¹⁷ I rebuked the nobles of Judah and said to them: "What is this evil you are doing—profaning the Sabbath day? ¹⁸ Didn't your ancestors do the same, so that our God brought all this disaster on us and on this city? And now you are rekindling [His] anger against Israel by profaning the Sabbath!"

¹⁹ When shadows began to fall on the gates of Jerusalem just before the Sabbath, I gave orders that the gates be closed and not opened until after the Sabbath. I posted some of my men at the gates, so that no goods could enter during the Sabbath day. ²⁰ Once or twice the merchants and those who sell all kinds of goods camped outside Jerusalem, ²¹ but I warned them, "Why are you camping in front of the wall? If you do it again, I'll use force against you." After that they did not come again on the Sabbath. ²² Then I instructed the Levites to purify themselves and guard the gates in order to keep the Sabbath day holy.

Remember me for this also, my God, and look on me with compassion in keeping with Your abundant, faithful love.

²³ In those days I also saw Jews who had married women from Ashdod, Ammon, and Moab. ²⁴ Half of their children spoke the language of Ashdod or of one of the other peoples but could not speak Hebrew. ²⁵ I rebuked them, cursed them, beat some of their men, and pulled out their hair. I forced them to take an oath before God and said: "You must not give your daughters in marriage to their sons or take their daughters as wives for your sons or yourselves! ²⁶ Didn't King Solomon of Israel sin in matters like this? There was not a king like him among many nations. He was loved by his God and God made him king over all Israel, yet foreign women drew him into sin. ²⁷ Why then should we hear about you doing all this terrible evil and acting unfaithfully against our God by marrying foreign women?"

²⁸ Even one of the sons of Jehoiada, son of Eliashib the high priest, had become a son-in-law to Sanballat the Horonite. So I drove him away from me.

²⁹ Remember them, my God, for defiling the priesthood as well as the covenant of the priesthood and the Levites.

³⁰ So I purified them from everything foreign and assigned specific duties to each of the priests and Levites. ³¹ I also arranged for the donation of wood at the appointed times and for the firstfruits.

Remember me, my God, with favor.

Nehemiah 13:4-31

Principles to Live By

The final chapter in Nehemiah's life story leaves us with two important perspectives on leadership. The first involves the appointment of qualified leaders, and the second involves dealing with sin in the lives of God's people.

Principle 1

IT IS IMPORTANT TO TURN OVER THE REINS OF LEADERSHIP TO SPIRITUALLY QUALIFIED, MATURE PEOPLE.

Nehemiah returned to Jerusalem to find that Eliashib the high priest had given Tobiah private quarters in the temple complex (vv. 4-5). Merchants were doing business on the Sabbath (v. 15). Leaders had failed to do anything about rampant intermarriage with pagans (vv. 23-24). Even the high priest's grandson had married an unbeliever (v. 28). Many of these leaders, such as the high priest and family elders, held hereditary positions. Nehemiah had no say over who filled those posts. He could, however, severely rebuke them (vv. 11, 17-18, 25-27). He also could appoint the managers who administered various programs and the workers who implemented them (vv. 13, 19b, 22a, 30-31a).

One spiritually unqualified leader can destroy years of work in a very short period of time. It simply takes one man with the power to make decisions to lead a multitude of people in the wrong direction. All he has to do is build around him a small group of like-minded people who share his own selfish and carnal agenda.

We need to be discerning about whom we entrust with leadership. We should seek wise counsel before making appointments. We should develop systems for screening potential leaders. Above all, we should faithfully seek God's will throughout our leadership selection process.

Some leaders find themselves unwilling to delegate authority because they are afraid to trust people. That isn't good. Ministry cannot grow apart from an expanding pool of qualified leaders. We have to find the balance between caution in selecting leaders and realizing that even the most trustworthy leader can fail at times.

Principle 2

ONE OF OUR GOD-GIVEN RESPONSIBILITIES AS LEADERS IS TO TEACH GOD'S TRUTH AND REVEALED WILL. WHEN PEOPLE VIOLATE HIS WILL AND DISHONOR GOD, WE ARE TO CONFRONT THAT DISOBEDIENCE WITH BIBLICAL TRUTH AS OUR BASIS.

LESSON 12

97

Nehemiah had to confront the people of Jerusalem and Judah over three areas of disobedience. These are important areas of sin and failure in the church today as well.

The first area of disobedience concerns dishonoring God through associations with those who don't follow Christ. We see this principle violated when Eliashib allowed Tobiah to live in the temple area (vv. 4-5). The children of Israel dramatically violated this when they encouraged marriage with people who did not believe in the one true God (v. 23).

Paul told the Corinthian Christians, "Do not be mismatched with unbelievers. For what partnership is there between righteousness and lawlessness? Or what fellowship does light have with darkness?" (2 Cor. 6:14). With this exhortation, Paul did not intend for us to isolate ourselves from non-Christians. Some of our greatest witnessing opportunities come when we're working side-by-side. What we must do, however, is to develop relationships that will influence us negatively and cause us to participate in sin. Two of the primary relationships to avoid are marriage and contractual business partnerships.

The second area of disobedience we should avoid is dishonoring God with our material possessions. According to the Law, Israel supported its priests and Levites through mandatory tithes and voluntary offerings from the crops and herds of all the people. When Nehemiah returned to Jerusalem from Susa, he found that the system of tithing had broken down (v. 10a). That is why the temple storeroom Tobiah took over had been empty (v. 5). That is why the Levites had abandoned their temple duties to get jobs to support themselves and their families (v. 10b).

Christians are not obligated to keep the Old Testament command to tithe, but the New Testament gives us several guidelines for giving to support God's work through the church:

1) We should give systematically. For instance, Paul encouraged the Corinthians to set aside their gifts on the first day of every week (1 Cor. 16:2).

2) We should give proportionately. If God has blessed us with wealth, we should give a greater amount and a higher percentage than believers who are less fortunate.

3) We should give cheerfully. God wants our giving to express a heart of gratitude and worship (2 Cor. 9:6-7). When we support the work of God, *we can expect God to meet our needs.* Jesus said, "But seek first the kingdom of God and His righteousness, and all these things will be provided for you" (Matt. 6:33). "All these things" refers to necessities, such as food and clothing (Matt. 6:25,31).

The third area of disobedience we should avoid is dishonoring God with our time. God had established the Sabbath as a day of rest for Israel (Ex. 20:8-11; Deut. 5:12-15). This rigid law was not to be violated in any way. The Jews of Jerusalem had corrupted the Sabbath in order to make money the same way their pagan neighbors did (Neh. 13:15-16). In the New Testament, however, God does not place us under this strict system. *Every day* is to be a special day for God.

Just as we can take advantage of God's grace because we aren't bound by the law of tithing, so we can ignore the important spiritual reality that motivated God to impose the original Sabbath regulation. God rested, and we should too (Ex. 20:11). God has freed us from bondage to sin, and we should not enslave ourselves to work or recreation (Deut. 5:15). We must not neglect to spend time in rest, worship, fellowship, and service (Heb. 10:24-25).

QUESTIONS FOR INTERACTION

1. How would you have felt if you had been Nehemiah discovering all your spiritual reforms had failed?

2. What does it say about Nehemiah's character that he didn't give up on the disobedient Jews?

3. How does this last chapter relate in time to the earlier chapters of Nehemiah (vv. 6-7)?

4. How did Eliashib the high priest and Tobiah earn Nehemiah's special anger (vv. 4-5, 7-9, 28)?

5. How did Nehemiah address the failure of the people to support the Levites with their tithes (vv. 10-13)?

6. How were the people violating the Sabbath (vv. 15-16)?

7. How did Nehemiah address the issue of Sabbath-breaking (vv. 17-22a)?

8. Why was Nehemiah so upset about intermarriage with unbelievers (vv. 23-28)?

9. Why do you suppose Nehemiah included so many prayers in his record of these events (vv. 14, 22b, 29, 31b)?

10. In what ways do you want to be like Nehemiah in this story of Scripture? In what ways do you want to avoid being like Nehemiah in this story of Scripture? Why?

GOING DEEPER

11. How can we recognize people who are qualified to be leaders in the church?

12. How can our churches help people know what God expects of them relative to associating with non-Christians, giving of their possessions, and building rest and worship into their weekly schedules?

13. How should the church confront and correct Christians who ignorantly or willfully disobey God's will in these three areas?

 ## CARING TIME

Perhaps you can identify with Nehemiah as you worry about whether you are succeeding as the spiritual leader of your family. Maybe you are engaged in a ministry that isn't growing as you had expected. Perhaps things aren't going well in your employment. Probably all of us have felt like walking away from some frustrating responsibility—or like punching somebody out or pulling their hair as Nehemiah did (v. 25)!

1. Why didn't Nehemiah just give up? Why shouldn't we when we face overwhelming frustration and stress?

2. What do you want God to remember you for as you persevere through the present frustrations of your life? How can you best express this to Him?

3. As we complete this study of the life of Nehemiah, what will be the major lessons you take away with you?

4. Let each man pray for at least one other group member that he will know God's power and approval as he deals with the present frustrations of his life.

SCRIPTURE NOTES

NEHEMIAH 13:4-31

13:5 prepared a large room ... stored the grain offerings. When Nehemiah returned to Jerusalem after an absence of several months, he discovered that the high priest Eliashib had allowed one of Nehemiah's enemies and his family to occupy one of the large temple storerooms used normally for storing grain offerings.

13:8 greatly displeased. Since Tobiah had opposed the restoration of the city walls, Nehemiah was angry that he had moved into the temple. He threw Tobiah's belongings out of the rooms, ordered that the rooms be cleaned, and refilled them with grain.

13:10 portions for the Levites had not been given. Nehemiah found that the people had not brought their tithes and offerings to support the temple as promised, forcing the Levites to work in the fields. He reprimanded the leaders for not enforcing the tithes and offerings.

13:13 they were considered trustworthy. Nehemiah appointed a priest, a scribe, a Levite, and an assistant to oversee the tithes of grain, new wine, and oil. He stationed the Levites at their proper posts. He knew that neglect could undo the reforms already accomplished.

13:17 rebuked the nobles of Judah. Another part of the written commitment was to honor the Sabbath (10:31). But in Jerusalem Nehemiah found the people carrying on trade on the Sabbath. He confronted the leaders who were responsible for enforcing the agreement.

13:19 When shadows began to fall. Nehemiah took action to stop trading on the Sabbath (Saturday) by shutting the city doors on Friday evening and posting guards. Days were counted from sunset to sunset. He coupled his action with prayer.

13:23 Jews who had married women from Ashdod, Ammon, and Moab. Ezra had dealt with the problem of intermarriage more than 25 years earlier (Ezra 9:1-4), and the people had made a covenant vow not to marry foreign wives again.

13:24 children spoke the language of Ashdod. Nehemiah knew that if the people did not speak and understand Hebrew, they could not learn the Law or worship in the temple. The Jews were raising children who did not know God.

13:25 You must not give your daughters in marriage. Nehemiah did not dissolve the foreign marriages like Ezra had done, but he reacted passionately, realizing that intermarriage was the sin that had led to Israel's captivity by Babylon.

13:26 King Solomon of Israel. Nehemiah reminded the people of Solomon, whose stellar beginning was ruined when he married foreign women (1 Kings 11:1-8).

drew him into sin. Solomon worshiped his foreign wives' idols, which drew his heart away from God. He even built high places to the false gods (1 Kings 11:7).

PERSONAL NOTES

ACKNOWLEDGMENTS

Creating a small-group study is an amazingly complex task, and is not just one man's effort. I truly appreciate the effective partnership between my team at the Center for Church Renewal and the team at Serendipity House, as well as all of the individuals who contributed to this effort.

I have been delighted to work with Joe Snider in developing my research and biblical principles into this Men of Purpose study. Joe was a student of mine in seminary, and now is a friend and gifted writer.

I am also deeply indebted to Iva Morelli and Sue Mitchell for their invaluable assistance in so many details of this and other projects. As always, my incredible wife and colaborer in life, Elaine has continued to motivate and encourage me.

My good friends at Serendipity House Publishing have again done a wonderful job in every aspect of this men's study. I especially want to thank publisher Ron Keck, editor in chief Ben Colter, art director Scott Lee, editor Cathy Tardif, along with the rest of the production team at Serendipity.

May God use this study to raise up some Nehemiahs in our day that will construct a vision of hope, demolish discouragement, and lead us to achieve great things for God's glory!

Other great resources from Serendipity House...

MORE

More depth, more meaning, more life.

Discovering truth through Bible study is much more than breaking a verse down to its smallest part and deconstructing a passage word by word. There is context and experience, mystery and story that all go into fully understanding the Word of God. By dissecting down to the smallest part, we often lose the essence of the whole. For this reason, Serendipity introduces a new approach to the inductive Bible-study format that looks at each passage within the context of the larger story. This reunifies the cognitive aspect with an experiential dynamic and allows the truths of scripture to come alive in new and unexpected ways.

Song of Songs: The Epic Romance 1574943405
Job: A Messy Faith 1574943464
Ruth: Gleaning Hope 141586702X

Mark: Beyond the Red Letters 1574943413
Colossians: Embrace the Mystery 1574944150

GOD AND THE ARTS

Where faith intersects life.

Stories, great and small, share the same essential structure because every story we tell borrows its power from a Larger Story. What we sense stirring within is a heart that is made for a place in the Larger Story. It is no accident that great movies include a hero, a villain, a betrayal, a battle to fight, a romance, and a beauty to rescue. It is The Epic Story and it is truer than anything we know. Adventure awaits. Listen.

Discover an experience that guides you on a journey into the one great Epic in which the Bible is set. These fun and provocative studies explore four films, each with two small-group meetings, _Dinner and a Movie_ (Week 1), _Connecting the Dots_ (Week 2), and an _Experience Guide_ that offers valuable insights.

Finding Jesus in the Movies 1574943553
Finding Redemption in the Movies 1574943421
Finding the Larger Story in Music 1574944207